3人执裁进阶
国际篮联裁判员手册

中国篮球协会 审定

北京体育大学出版社

策划编辑：曾　莉
责任编辑：曾　莉　李　涛
责任校对：张志富
版式设计：高文函

图书在版编目（CIP）数据

国际篮联裁判员手册. 3人执裁进阶 / 中国篮球协会审定. -- 北京：北京体育大学出版社，2021.9（2024.11重印）
　ISBN 978-7-5644-3495-3

Ⅰ. ①国… Ⅱ. ①中… Ⅲ. ①篮球运动—裁判法—手册 Ⅳ. ① G841.4-62

中国版本图书馆 CIP 数据核字 (2021) 第 189990 号

国际篮联裁判员手册：3人执裁进阶　　　　中国篮球协会　审定

出版发行：北京体育大学出版社
地　　址：北京市海淀区农大南路1号院2号楼2层办公B-212
邮　　编：100084
网　　址：http://cbs.bsu.edu.cn
发 行 部：010-62989320
邮 购 部：北京体育大学出版社读者服务部 010-62989432
印　　刷：河北盛世彩捷印刷有限公司
开　　本：880mm×1230mm　　　1/32
成品尺寸：145mm×210mm
印　　张：3.75
字　　数：104千字
版　　次：2021年11月第1版
印　　次：2024年11月第3次印刷
定　　价：28.00元

（本书如有印刷质量问题，请与出版社联系调换）
版权所有·侵权必究

出版说明

- 《国际篮联裁判员手册：3 人执裁进阶》由中国篮球协会依照国际篮球联合会（简称"国际篮联"）发布的 FIBA Referees Manual 翻译和修订。今后所有正式国际篮球比赛和国内篮球比赛，以及各类篮球裁判员晋级考试，均按最新《篮球规则》及《国际篮联裁判员手册》执行。

- 《国际篮联裁判员手册：3 人执裁进阶》的翻译和编订力求忠实于原文。如在理解和执行过程中出现争议，以国际篮联官方语言英文版为准。翻译和审校工作可能存在疏漏之处，欢迎广大读者提出意见和建议，以便我们及时修订和完善。

- 整本《国际篮联裁判员手册：3 人执裁进阶》中所有提到的教练员、运动员、技术官员等都是男性，同样也适用于女性。必须强调，这样写只是为了实用的缘故。

FOREWORD

Basketball, as a game, is progressing in skill and speed every day. It is a natural environmental development process that takes place unconditionally and it is called evolution. The game and more so refereeing has completely changed from 10 years ago. Presently, top level refereeing is improving at least at the same speed as the game itself and higher standards of performance are expected every year. The pace of change has necessitated the adoption of a motto: "What was considered exceptionally good yesterday, is considered standard quality today and below average quality tomorrow".

This FIBA Advanced 3 Person Officiating Manual presents more in depth mechanics for successful basketball refereeing at the elite level. To successfully operate in higher levels of basketball, referees are expected to train and use these mechanics in all games. To use the advanced content, referees are required to first master the FIBA Basic 3PO Manual knowledge in order to build a solid and lasting foundation.

This advanced manual complements other FIBA technical manuals for officiating. FIBA basic technical manuals offer entry level training content for minimum standards of FIBA officiating, while FIBA Advanced technical manuals give a more in-depth look and are targeted to a more advanced group of referees. Advanced materials include all the same information that can be found in a Basic Manual plus additional and more detailed instructions on the subject. It is important for referees to refer to the most appropriate manual based upon their existing skill level.

In addition, the FIBA Referee Operations produces a variety of supporting material, namely "Improve Your…" series (for example 'Improve Your… Rotation'). These brief guides provide more insight and details on how to work with the content mentioned in this manual.

In the case of a discrepancy between any guidelines in the Manual and the Official Basketball Rules (OBR) and/or the Official Basketball Rules Interpretations (OBRI), the latter (OBR and OBRI) will prevail.

前 言

篮球作为一项运动，在技术和速度方面每天都在进步，它是一种自然发展过程，无条件发生，被称为演变。比赛本身以及执裁方式与10年前完全不同。目前，顶级的执裁方式的进展速度快于篮球比赛本身，并且每年都有更高的裁判规范标准。目前的发展速度使我们树立了一个座右铭："过去被视为极好的标准，在当前是普通标准，到了将来会低于平均标准。"

《国际篮联裁判员手册：3人执裁进阶》为精英级别的成功执裁提供了更加深入的指导原则。为在更高水平的篮球比赛中成功应用，裁判需要在所有比赛中训练和使用这些裁判法。要使用进阶的内容，裁判员必须首先掌握《国际篮联裁判员手册：3人执裁进阶》中的知识，并建立牢固的和持久的基础。

这本《国际篮联裁判员手册：3人执裁进阶》是对其他国际篮联执裁技术手册的补充。《国际篮联裁判员手册：3人执裁基础》提供了入门级的国际篮联执裁标准的训练内容，而《国际篮联裁判员手册：3人执裁进阶》给予更多深入剖析，并针对更高阶的裁判团队。进阶手册包括可以在基础手册中找得到的所有相同的信息，并且加上关于该主题的其他和更详细的指导。根据裁判员的现有技能水平来参考最合适的手册，这对他们来说是很重要的。

此外，国际篮联裁判运营部提供各种配套支持材料，比如"提高你的……"系列（例如"提高你的……轮转"）。这些简要指南提供了更多关于如何使用本手册内容的见解和细节。

如果本手册的任何指导方针与官方《篮球规则》和/或官方《篮球规则解释》有不一致之处，以后者（官方《篮球规则》和/或《官方篮球规则》）解释为准。

TABLE OF CONTENTS

CHAPTER 1

1.	INTRODUCTION & GENERAL	2
1.1	BASKETBALL OFFICIATING	2
1.2	IMAGE OF AN ELITE BASKETBALL REFEREE	2

CHAPTER 2

2.	ADVANCED THREE PERSON OFFICIATING	8
2.1	INTRODUCTION	8
2.2	BASIC BASKETBALL OFFICIATING TERMINOLOGY	8
2.3	SYMBOLS USED	10
2.4	GENERAL COURT POSITIONS	12
2.5	PRE-GAME / HALF-TIME POSITIONS	16
2.6	JUMP BALL & START OF THE QUARTERS	16
2.7	COURT COVERAGE	20
2.8	ROTATION	24
2.9	LEAD POSITION & TRANSITION	36
2.10	TRAIL POSITION & TRANSITION	42
2.11	CENTRE POSITION & TRANSITION	46
2.12	FAST BREAK	52
2.13	PRESS DEFENCE	54
2.14	OUT-OF-BOUNDS & THROW-INS	56
2.15	SHOT COVERAGE (GENERAL & 3 POINTS ATTEMPTS)	58
2.16	TIME-OUTS	60
2.17	SUBSTITUTIONS	64
2.18	EIGHT SECONDS & BACKCOURT VIOLATIONS	64
2.19	SHOT CLOCK COVERAGE	66
2.20	BASKET INTERFERENCE & GOALTENDING	66
2.21	REPORTING FOULS & SWITCHING	70
2.22	FREE THROW COVERAGE	84
2.23	REBOUNDING COVERAGE	88
2.24	LAST SHOT	90

CHAPTER 3

3.	OFFICIAL REFEREES' SIGNALS	96

目录

第 1 章

1.	**导论与通则**	**3**
1.1	篮球比赛执裁	3
1.2	精英篮球裁判员的形象	3

第 2 章

2.	**3 人执裁进阶**	**9**
2.1	引言	9
2.2	基础篮球执裁术语	9
2.3	使用的符号	11
2.4	通常的场上位置	13
2.5	赛前和半时的位置	17
2.6	跳球和每节的开始	17
2.7	场上的区域分工	21
2.8	轮转	25
2.9	前导裁判的位置和攻防转换	37
2.10	追踪裁判的位置和攻防转换	43
2.11	中央裁判的位置和攻防转换	47
2.12	快攻	53
2.13	紧逼防守	55
2.14	球出界与掷球入界	57
2.15	投篮的区域分工（一般情况与 3 分试投）	59
2.16	暂停	61
2.17	替换	65
2.18	8 秒违例与球回后场违例	65
2.19	进攻计时钟的区域分工	67
2.20	干扰得分与干涉得分	67
2.21	报告犯规与换位	71
2.22	罚球的区域分工	85
2.23	篮板球的区域分工	89
2.24	最后一投	91

第 3 章

3.	**官方裁判员手势**	**97**

国际篮联裁判员手册
3人执裁进阶
（英文版）

第 1 章

INTRODUCTION & GENERAL

导论与通则

CHAPTER 1

1. INTRODUCTION & GENERAL

1.1 BASKETBALL OFFICIATING

Generally, sports officiating is challenging and more so in the game of basketball – especially where ten athletic players are moving fast in a restricted area. Naturally the game has changed and the court has actually become larger, not in actual court size but in the playing and refereeing sense. Play situations are spread all over the court with every player able to play in almost every position. Naturally this sets a new requirement for basketball refereeing. It is good to remember that improving daily should not be considered as actual progress but rather is only designed to keep pace with the game's development – this is called evolution and this will occur regardless if we want it or not.

Sometimes there is a tendency to define basketball officiating as a very complex combination of various skills. It is true it requires many abilities by the referee, but the bottom line is that all these skills aim to achieve one thing – being ready to referee the play or handle situations that may arise during the game.

Refereeing is:
Anticipate what will happen — Active mind-set
Understand what is happening — Basketball knowledge
React properly for what has happened — Mental Image Training

1.2 IMAGE OF AN ELITE BASKETBALL REFEREE

FIBA has one golden rule when it comes to prioritising referee training for FIBA games – Game Control. The intent is to ensure a smooth running and dynamic game where players are able to showcase their basketball skills. This is the image FIBA is looking for. The two or three appointed referees are the ones who are responsible for this game control.

第1章

1. 导论与通则

1.1 篮球比赛执裁

一般而言,执裁体育比赛是十分具有挑战性的,在篮球比赛中更是如此——特别是当 10 名运动员在有限的空间范围内快速移动时。自然而然地,比赛就发生了很多变化,比赛场地实际上变大了。这不是篮球场的实际大小发生变化,而是对比赛和执裁的意义上而言的。对抗的情况遍布全场,每个队员几乎都能在任何位置上进行比赛。自然,这为篮球裁判的工作提出了新的要求。最好记住,日常业务改进和提高难以被称为业务能力的进步,而只是作为跟上篮球运动发展节奏的必备条件。这就是所谓的进步,并且无论我们同意与否,都会发生这种改变。

有这样一种趋势,将执裁篮球比赛定义为一项包含多种不同复杂技能的综合体。确实,它需要裁判员具备多项能力。但底线是,所有技能都旨在达成一个目标,准备好执裁比赛或处理好比赛中可能出现的情况。

执裁是:

预测场上将要发生什么——动态思维
理解场上正在发生什么——篮球知识
恰当反映已经发生什么——心理训练

1.2 精英篮球裁判员的形象

在国际篮联的裁判员培训中心有一项优先进行的内容,也就是国际篮联的黄金法则——比赛控制。目的是为了确保比赛能够流畅顺利且具有活力地进行,以便让运动员能够充分展示自己的篮球技能,这是国际篮联希望发生的情况。归根结底,裁判员要对比赛负责。他们定义了什么是允许的,什么是不允许的,谁都不例外。

It is good to define and remember that game control is different to game management. Ultimately, it is the Referees that are in charge of the game. They define what is allowed and what is not – nobody else.

Having said that, it is equally important that referees look and act like they are in charge. Referees should give a non-verbal message that they are ready and able to make decisions. The core function of refereeing is decision making. Referees need to feel comfortable in making decisions without hesitation in the decision making process. Of course, the correctness of these decisions can be analysed after the event and so referees must demonstrate confidence and trust or at the very least present so that others view them this way (perception).

Therefore, FIBA has added the topic of "court presence" to its training program. It includes mental training with an "I am in charge" concept. This will be combined with a physical training plan to create an image of a strong and athletic body, fitting into the image of professionalism and promoting game control.

"Controlling is an attitude"

记住控制比赛和管理比赛是不同的。最终,裁判员要对比赛负责——绝不是其他人。他们定义什么是允许的,什么是不被允许的。

行文至此,裁判员的形象和举止也是同样重要的。裁判员应当以非语言的信号来表现出自己已经做好准备并且能够很好地执裁比赛。执裁的核心要义是决策。裁判员需要在决策过程中毫不犹豫地做出决定。当然,这些决定的正确与否可以在赛后进行分析总结。因此,裁判员必须表现出自信和信任,或者至少是在当下,让其他人看起来他们是这样的。

因此,国际篮联在训练计划中增加了"赛场仪容仪表"的课题。它包含了以"我在执裁"为核心的心理表象训练内容。这将与体能训练计划相结合,打造一个强壮的运动型身体形象,以适应专业形象并提升对比赛的控制。

"控制是一种态度"

第 2 章

ADVANCED THREE PERSON OFFICIATING

3人执裁进阶

CHAPTER 2

2. ADVANCED THREE PERSON OFFICIATING

2.1 INTRODUCTION

Three referees is the best way to have an elite level game officiated. If it was not, the NBA, WNBA, NCAA, FIBA and all of the top leagues in the world would not use this system. In modern basketball, the game is spread all over the court and multiple actions take place simultaneously. 3PO is a great tool to implement correct IOT principles and to provide more time to actually process the play analytically (start-middle-end of the play) before making a decision. The analyses show that correct "no calls" are higher with 3PO than 2PO, and first illegal actions are called rather than reactions. These both actually decrease the number of calls and allow for a more dynamic game.

The key to successful 3PO is one simple word: trust. You must trust your partners. Only then can you concentrate on your primary area of coverage, and not have to worry about what is going on in your partner's area. Ideally, all three referees should have one primary in 3PO and there should be no need to referee any secondary coverage.

At the top level of officiating, 3PO is seamless teamwork where all three referees are individually refereeing where the others cannot, each covering part of the court, or at the advanced level, covering a different part of the very same play. However, before progressing to an advanced level, it is important to have a solid knowledge and understanding of 3PO basics.

2.2 BASIC BASKETBALL OFFICIATING TERMINOLOGY

Basic terms used in all FIBA Manuals can be found in "Basic basketball officiating terminology" publication. It can be downloaded from FIBA iRef Academy Library App. It is advisable to know these terms and their meaning before studying the material.

第 2 章

2.3 人执裁进阶

2.1 引言

三名裁判员执法是执裁一场精英级别比赛的最佳形式。若非如此，NBA、WNBA、NCAA、FIBA等世界顶级联赛也不会在比赛中使用这种形式。现代篮球中，由于比赛的活动范围遍及整个球场，再加上多重动作同时发生。3人执裁是一种很好的去正确运用个人执裁技术原则的方法，而且在做出决定前为准确分析处理比赛（动作开始—发展—结束的全过程）提供了更多时间。分析表明，3人执裁中正确的"不宣判"情况要比2人执裁更多，并且对于非法的第一动作要做出宣判而不只是反应。这些不仅减少了鸣哨判罚的次数同时也保障了更流畅的比赛。

成功的3人执裁关键要点是：信任。你必须相信你的同伴。只有这样，你才能够集中注意力于你的主要责任区，而不会去关心你的同伴的责任区里发生了什么。理想的情况下，3人执裁时三名裁判员都应有自己的主要责任区，同时也不必要去关注任何的次要责任区。

在高水平的执裁中，3人执裁是一种密切配合的团队活动，需要三名裁判员互相配合去观察比赛场地的各个部分，甚至在更高级别的比赛中去观察同一个动作的不同部分。然而，在提升到更高级别的过程中，掌握扎实的理论以及理解3人执裁的基础也很重要。

2.2 基础篮球执裁术语

在已发布的"基础篮球执裁术语"中可查阅到所有的国际篮联手册里出现的基本术语。这些可在FIBA iRef Academy Library App中下载。建议在学习本书前理解相关术语及其内容含义。

2.3 SYMBOLS USED

SYMBOL	EXPLANATION
T L C	Trail referee or "T", in green colour on diagrams. Lead referee or "L", in blue colour on diagrams. Centre referee or "C", in red colour on diagrams. The base of the triangle represents the facing direction of the referee.
T L C (grey)	Previous positions of Trail, Lead and Centre. Same principle (grey=previous) is applied to all symbols (ball, players etc.).
CC U1 U2	Crew Chief (CC), Umpire 1 (U1), Umpire 2 (U2)
➔	Direction of the play
⇢ ⇢ ⇢	Direction of the Trail (green), Lead (blue) and Centre (red) referee
🔔	Referee blowing the whistle
✹	Action Spot - Foul Called
(cone)	Coverage area
(framed referee)	Reporting referee indicated by the frame colour (T=green, L=blue, C=red)
A1 B1	Player A1 (offensive player), B1 (defensive player)
∿∿∿➔	Dribble

2.3 使用的符号

符号	注释
T L C	追踪裁判或"T",图示为绿色 前导裁判或"L",图示为蓝色 中央裁判或"C",图示为红色 三角形的底边代表裁判员面向的方向
T L C	灰色代表追踪裁判、前导裁判和中央裁判 相同的准则(灰色的=先前的)适用于所有的符号 (包括球、队员等)
CC U1 U2	主裁判(CC),第一副裁判(U1),第二副裁判(U2)
→	比赛方向
⇢⇢⇢	追踪裁判(绿色),前导裁判(蓝色)和中央裁判(红色)的移动方向
🎺	裁判员鸣哨
✷	动作发生地点——宣判犯规
◁	视野覆盖区域
🃏	边框的颜色表示正在报告的裁判员 (T=绿色,L=蓝色,C=红色)
A1 B1	队员A1(进攻队员),B1(防守队员)
∿→	运球

2.4 GENERAL COURT POSITIONS

Target: Understand the basic court positions of Trail, Lead and Centre in 3PO, and positions before the game and during the time-outs.

Let's start with some key terms regarding the court positions.

TERM	EXPLANATION
Strong side –refereeing (SSR)	Side of the court where the Lead & Trail referees are located (in 3PO).
Weak side –refereeing (WSR)	Side of the court where the Centre referee is located (in 3PO).
Ball-side (BS)	This refers to the position of the ball. When the playing court is divided by an imaginary line extending from basket to basket, the side of the playing court on which the ball is located is called the "ball-side".
Help side (HSB)	The half of the front court opposite to where the ball is located.
Table side (TS)	This refers to the side of the playing court which is closest to the scorer's table.
Opposite side (OPS)	This refers to the side of the playing court which is furthest away from the scorer's table.
Trail (T)	The Trail is the referee who is positioned approximately at the edge of the team bench area nearer to the centre line and on the same side as the L (always strong side) and who stands behind the play.
Lead (L)	The Lead is the referee who is positioned at the endline. The Lead should be always on the ball-side as much of possible (strong side).
Centre (C)	The Centre is the referee who is positioned on the opposite side of the frontcourt from the L (usually opposite ball-side) at the free-throw line extended (set-up position). Depending on the location of the ball, C may be on either side of the frontcourt. Standard working area for C is on the court.

2.4 通常的场上位置

目标：理解 3 人执裁中追踪裁判、前导裁判和中央裁判基本的场上位置，以及比赛开始前和暂停期间的位置。

先依据场上的位置了解一些重要的术语。

术语	注释
强侧－执裁（SSR）	前导裁判与追踪裁判所在一侧的场地（3 人执裁时）
弱侧－执裁（WSR）	中央裁判所在一侧的场地（3 人执裁时）
球侧（BS）	此术语涉及球的位置。在两个球篮间用一条假想的线将球场划分为两部分，球所在的场地一侧为"球侧"
协助侧（HSB）	球所在前场场地的对面一侧
记录台侧（TS）	指靠近记录台的场地一侧
对侧（OPS）	指远离记录台的场地一侧
追踪裁判（T）	追踪裁判是大约落位于靠近中线的球队席区域边界的裁判员，同时与 L 在同一侧（强侧），并且位于比赛的后方
前导裁判（L）	前导裁判是落位于端线的裁判员。他的位置应始终尽最大可能地位于球侧（强侧）
中央裁判（C）	中央裁判是落位于 L 所在前场的对侧的裁判员（通常在球侧对面），在（初始位置）罚球线延长线。根据球的位置，C 可以位于前场的任意一侧。C 的标准工作区域在场地内

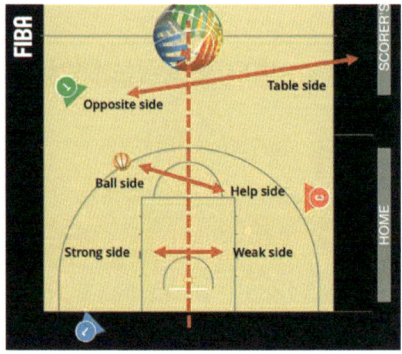

Diagram 1:
Trail, Lead, Centre, Strong-side, Weak side, Ball-side, Help side, Table side and Opposite side.

The whole idea of 3PO is based on the concept that two referees (T & L) are on ball side as much as possible. This gives them at least two different angles on ball side play situations and analyses has demonstrated that this leads to higher decision making accuracy. To achieve this during the game the referees need to adjust their triangle by rotating (see *"2.8 Rotation"*).

Diagram 2:
Front court basic positions for Trail, Lead and Centre when the L is located on the table-side.

Diagram 3:
Front court basic positions for Trail, Lead and Centre when the L is located on opposite-side.

图1：
追踪裁判（T）、前导裁判（L）、中央裁判（C）、强侧、弱侧、球侧、协助侧、记录台侧和对侧

3人执裁的整体理念是将两名裁判员（T&L）尽可能保持在球侧。这提供两个不同视角观察球侧的比赛情况。通过分析已经表明，这可以有效地提高执裁的准确性。为了在比赛中实现这一目标，裁判员需通过不断地轮转来调整其三人的三角形位置。（见"2.8 轮转"）。

图2：
当L在记录台同侧时，前场的追踪裁判、前导裁判和中央裁判的初始位置

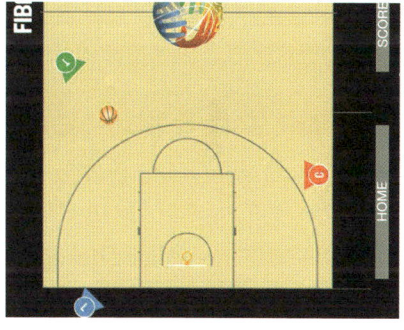

图3：
当L落位于对侧时，前场的追踪裁判、前导裁判和中央裁判的初始位置

2.5 PRE-GAME / HALF-TIME POSITIONS

The standard positioning before the game and during the half-time is described in Diagram 4.

If the referees are warming-up properly, one referee observes the court while the other two warm-up on the outside of the sideline (Diagram 5). The referees should rotate into different positions in order to have a proper warm-up and to observe the teams. More on this subject in "Improve Your... Game Warm Up & Streching"publication.

Diagram 4:
Standard pre-game position.

Diagram 5:
Optional pre-game position when two referees can warm-up all the time.

2.6 JUMP BALL & START OF THE QUARTERS

Target: To identify and understand the procedures during the opening jump ball and start of the quarters.

The position of the referees during the opening jump-ball:

1. The Crew Chief (CC) is responsible for tossing the jump ball from a position facing the scorer's table.

2. The umpires take positions on the opposite sidelines. U1 is table-side close to midcourt line and U2 is opposite side, near the edge of the team bench area.

3. U1 responsibilities:
    a. Calling for a re-jump on a poor toss or a jumper violation.
    b. Giving the time-in signal to start the game clock when ball is legally tapped.

2.5 赛前和半时的位置

图 4 展示了比赛前和半场时裁判员的标准位置。

如果裁判员要进行适当的热身，应当留一名裁判员观察场上情况，另外两名裁判员在边线外进行热身（图 5）。裁判员可以交替热身，并保持观察球队情况。详细内容见已发布的"改进你的……赛前热身与拉伸"。

图 4：
比赛前裁判员标准站位

图 5：
赛前两名裁判员热身时的可选位置

2.6 跳球和每节的开始

目标：确认和理解跳球和每节比赛开始的程序。

开场跳球时裁判员的位置：

1. 主裁判（CC）负责从面对记录台的位置跳球抛球。
2. 两名副裁判站在相对的两条边线位置。U1 站在记录台侧靠近中场位置的边线，U2 站在对侧的球队席界线的位置。
3. U1 的责任：
   a. 在抛球不好时宣判重新跳球或者跳球队员违例。
   b. 当球被合法拍击时，做出开动比赛计时钟的手势。

4. U2 responsibility: observing the eight (8) non-jumpers for possible violations and fouls.

Diagram 6:
The Crew Chief administers the toss and U1 is located close to midcourt line to observe possible poor toss and violations by jumpers, U2 is located opposite site observing the possible violations by non-jumpers.

Jump ball – play goes to Crew Chief's left

Diagram 7:
1) U1 becomes L, 2) U2 becomes C, 3) The Crew Chief moves to the sideline where was U1 and become T.

Jump ball – play goes to Crew Chief's right

Diagram 8:
1) U2 becomes L, 2) U1 becomes C, 3) The Crew Chief (CC) moves to the sideline where was U2 and become T.

4. U2 的责任：观察其他 8 名非跳球队员，是否能出现违例与犯规。

图 6：
主裁判执行抛球，U1 位于靠近中线的位置观察可能存在的抛球失误或跳球队员违例，U2 位于场地对侧观察非跳球队员可能出现的违例

跳球后比赛向主裁判左侧发展

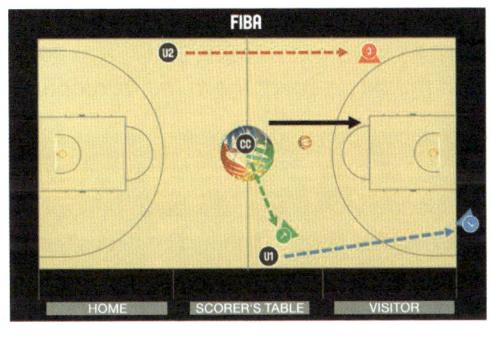

图 7：
1）U1 变成 L，2）U2 变成 C，3）主裁判移动到之前 U1 的边线位置变成 T

跳球后比赛向主裁判右侧移动

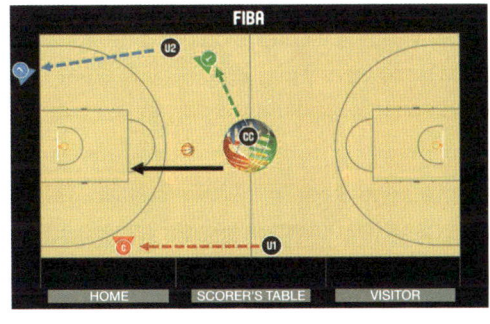

图 8：
1）U2 变成 L，2）U1 变成 C，3）主裁判（CC）移动到之前 U2 的边线位置变成 T

Start of the 2nd, 3rd & 4th quarter and overtime:

The positioning of the referees is 1) The Crew Chief (CC) administers the throw-in at midcourt and becomes T 2) U1/U2 position themselves in L position opposite-side and in C position table-side.

Diagram 9:
The Crew Chief will always be the administering referee for the throw-in opposite-side to start the quarters. U1 and U2 will place themselves either in L or C position.

2.7 COURT COVERAGE

Target: To identify and understand the basic coverage in the frontcourt.

When 3PO works optimally with experienced, professional referees, they will only need to officiate in their own primaries. If all three referees cover their primaries, there is in theory no need for any secondary coverage. The basic principle is that a referee should have an open look on the play, and should be in position to referee an area which the other two referees are unable to observe.

In the diagrams below, the Lead has the smallest area of coverage by size, but the analyses clearly indicate that the Lead still makes about 50-60% of all foul calls in the game. This is the result of the so called "action area" (also known as "bus-station") which is the post on the ball-side. In other words, most of the plays end up in the action area and if Lead is on ball-side, as Lead should be, he/she has the best angle to cover any play in the action area. This is why it is critical to have two referees (T & L = strong side) on ball side as much as possible.

Naturally, the game is dynamic but coverage areas in theory are static. This is why there are two different descriptions of the coverage areas: Principle (static – Diagram 10 & Diagram 11) and Functional (dynamic - Diagram 12 & Diagram 13) which will have naturally overlapping or dual coverage in the same primary.

第 2 节、第 3 节、第 4 节和决胜期比赛的开始：

裁判员的站位是：1）主裁判（CC）在中线处管理掷球入界并成为T，2）U1／U2分别落位于对侧L和记录台侧C的位置。

图 9：
主裁判总是成为在每节比赛开始时管理对侧掷球入界的裁判员。U1和U2可以落位于任一L或C的位置

2.7 场上的区域分工

目标：区分和理解在前场的基本区域分工。

当富有经验的职业的裁判员密切配合进行3人执裁时，他们只需要执裁自己的主要责任区。如果三名裁判员每一名都观察他们的主要责任区，那么也就不需要任何的次要责任区。基本的原则是一名裁判员应该有开放的视野去注视一个动作，同时也应处于能够执裁到其他两名裁判员所无法观察的区域的位置。

根据下图所示，前导裁判的责任区在面积上是最小的，但是分析表明他仍然吹罚了50%~60%的犯规。这可被叫做"动态区"（也被称为"公交站"），指在球侧的低位区。换言之，绝大多数的动作会在动态区终结。若前导裁判位于球侧，也本应在此侧，那么他/她应该有最好的角度去观察动态区的任何动作。这也就是球侧应该尽可能有两名裁判员（T与L＝强侧）的关键性原因。

通常来说，比赛是经常变化的，但区域分工在理论上是固定的。这就是为什么会出现对区域分工的两种描述：静态（固定的——图10与图11）以及动态（变化的——图12与图13），主要责任区自然会出现重叠位置以及共管区域。

Diagram 10:
Court coverage in principle by all T, L and C when the L is located on the table-side.

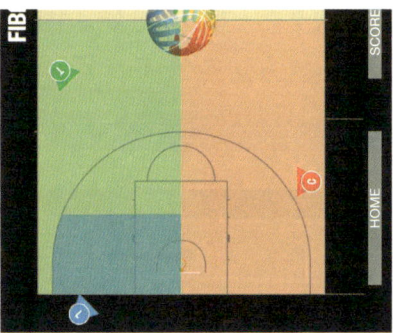

Diagram 11:
Court coverage in principle by all T, L and C when the L is located on opposite-side.

Diagram 12:
The functional court coverage by all T, L and C when the L is located on the table-side.

Diagram 13:
The functional court coverage by all T, L and C when the L is located on opposite-side.

图 10:
当 L 位于记录台侧时, T、L 和 C 的责任区域(静态)

图 11:
当 L 位于对侧时, T、L 和 C 的责任区域(静态)

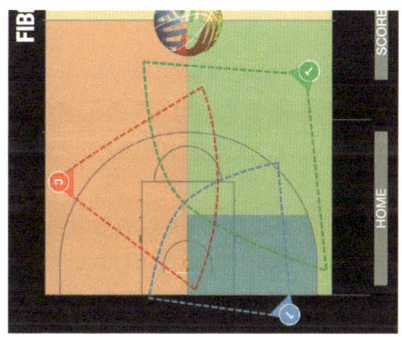

图 12:
当 L 位于记录台侧时, T、L 和 C 的责任区域(动态)

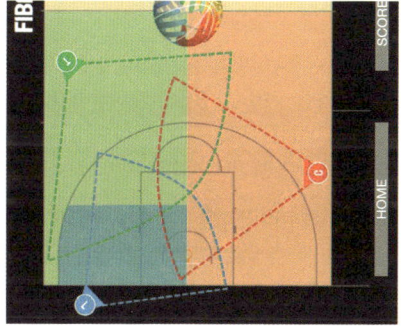

图 13:
当 L 位于对侧时, T、L 和 C 的责任区域(动态)

2.8 ROTATION

Target: To identify the need, time and proper techniques of rotation.

The successful outcome of 3PO depends on how many of the play situations involving the ball are covered by the strong side referees (L & T). For that reason, 3PO has rotational movements that allows the Lead to change the position (rotate) on the endline to the other side of the court.

Lead always initiates and dictates the rotation. It is very important that Lead is always looking for reasons to rotate (not reasons not to rotate). This active mind-set keeps 3PO coverage active in the frontcourt ensuring two referees are on ball side as much as possible. While it may appear to those who do not have experience with 3PO that the referees are just moving in rotation and that it is not important how the rotation is executed, it should be understood there is a specific technique in each position during the rotation. L, T & C must constantly be aware of when & how to rotate, and when to switch their area of coverage.

The keys to the successful technique of a proper rotation, especially by L who initiates it, are (1) proper distance to rotate (close down), (2) proper timing to rotate (when ball moves to the weak side), and (3) proper technique (assess, move sharply, no hesitation).

During some games analysed, it has been identified that more play situations have ended up with a drive or a shot from the weak side rather than from the strong side, meaning that only one referee (C) has ball coverage. This is contrary to the philosophy and meaning of 3PO.

When analysing the rotations at the advanced level, we should always consider whether a rotation was possible in the case of a weak side shot and/or drive. If the answer is yes, then there is room to improve. But first it is crucial to learn to understand the concept of rotation and basic techniques to be able to execute effectively.

Rotation in summary:

1. Ball moves to the middle of the court (Zone/Rectangle 2) -> Lead closes down.

2.8 轮转

目标：明确轮转的需要、时机和恰当的技巧。

3人执裁运用的成功与否，取决于前导裁判和追踪裁判能够负责多少球侧的比赛情况L&T。就是由于这个原因，3人执裁才会有轮转，使得前导裁判从端线的一侧移动到另一侧（轮转）。

轮转总是由前导裁判发起。因此，前导裁判总是在不断寻找发动或中断轮转的理由（没有理由就不轮转）。这种保持活跃的精神状态，得以使强侧和球侧能够尽可能地重合，但在一些没有3人执裁经验的人来看，裁判员只是轮转移动，轮转是如何执行的就没那么重要了，应该了解轮转中每一个位置都有特殊的技术。前导裁判、追踪裁判和中央裁判要持续地意识到什么时候进行轮转，如何轮转以及如何转换他们的责任区。

恰当的轮转技术，尤其是前导裁判发动轮转的信号，成功的关键，是（1）恰当的距离（轮转发动区）；（2）恰当的时机（当球运行到弱侧）；（3）恰当的技巧(预判、快速移动、毫不犹豫）。

在分析一些比赛时，发现更多的比赛情况是以在弱侧而非强侧的突破和投篮结束的。这就意味着在有球区域只有一个中央裁判监控。这和3人执裁的精神和意图相反。

在分析高级别轮转时，我们应该总是考虑到当弱侧投篮或突破时轮转是否可能，如果答案是可能，那么就有改善的空间。但是首先，至关重要的是要学会理解轮转的概念和执行轮转的基本技术。

轮转的步骤：

1. 球位于靠近中场的位置（中间区域、2区）→前导裁判位于轮转发动点。

FIBA REFEREES MANUAL

2. Ball moves to the weak side (outside Zone/Rectangle 2) -> A) Lead rotates to the weak side and B) Trail rotates to the new Centre position.

3. Lead has completed the rotation and is ready to referee the play -> Centre rotates to the new Trail position. Rotation is completed.

4. When there is a quick shot or a drive from the weak side, there should be no rotation initiated by Lead (see Phase 2a –Pause).

5. When rotating, Lead walks sharply (never runs). This allows Lead to abort the rotation in the case of a quick shot or drive from the weak side, or a change in the direction of the play.

Rotation has 4 different phases:

1. **Phase 1: Close Down** When the ball is in the middle of the court (rectangle 2), Lead should move to the close down position in order to be ready to rotate when the ball moves to the weak side (outside of rectangle 2).

If ball returns back to the strong side, Lead will kick out to the normal set-up position.

Note: Close down position is not the position to referee the play. If there is a drive to the basket or a shot, Lead in close down position should move out in order to have proper distance and angle for the play.

Diagram 14:
Ball moves and remains at rectangle 2 – Lead moves to close down position.

Diagram 15:
If ball moves back to the strong side – Lead moves back to the initial position.

2. 球移动到弱侧（超越了中间区域/2区）→A）前导裁判轮转到弱侧，B）追踪裁判变成新的中央裁判。

3. 前导裁判已经完成轮转并做好了执裁比赛的准备→中央裁判变成新的追踪裁判，轮转完成。

4. 当在弱侧出现快速投篮或突破时，前导裁判不需要发动轮转（见"第二阶段a——暂停"）。

5. 当轮转时，前导裁判要快走（不要跑）。这使他可以在弱侧出现快速投篮、突破或攻防转换时，可以终止轮转。

轮转有4个不同的阶段：

1. **第一阶段：轮转发动点** 当球在球场中央（2区）时，前导裁判应该移动到轮转发动点位置，以做好球移动到弱侧（超越了2区）的准备。

   如果球回到强侧，前导裁判就退回到起始位置。

   注意：轮转发动点位置不是执裁比赛的位置，如果有上篮或投篮，为了有一个合适的距离和角度，在轮转发动点的前导裁判需要移出来。

图14：
球移动到2区，前导裁判移动到轮转发动点位置

图15：
如果球移动回强侧——前导裁判回到其初始位置

2. **Phase 2: Rotation by Lead & Trail** When the ball moves to the weak side, Lead starts the rotation as soon as possible. At the same time, Trail moves into the new Centre position.

    a. **Phase 2a: Rotation by Lead – Pause** When the ball has arrived to the weak side, the Lead should analyse if there is a chance for a quick shot or a drive from the weak side. This one second ("one breath") delay is called Pause. If a player with the ball takes a shot or drives to the basket, there will be no rotation and the Centre needs to cover the play on the weak side. Why – the principles of distance & stationary refereeing an individual play still need to be respected (above all).

    b. **Phase 2b: Rotation by Lead – Scan** the Paint When rotating, Lead should walk straight and sharply, while actively refereeing all the time. If there are players in the paint, they are Lead's primary and if not, Lead looks for the next active matchup(s) or players that might arrive to the action area (bus station) on the new strong side.

Diagram 16:
Ball moves to the middle of the court, L closes down. C prepares to start covering on the ball.

Diagram 17:
Ball moves to the weak side, L rotates and scans the paint or closest match-up.

    c. **Phase 2c: Rotation by Trail to Centre position** As soon as the Trail has ensured that the Centre has picked up the ball on the weak side, the Trail should re-focus their vision and pick up the new weak side post play before starting the rotation. Studies have indicated that this is one of the weakest links during the rotation procedure, because often Trail remains locked in with the ball whilst rotating and without first re-focusing vision onto the weak side action.

2. **第二阶段：前导裁判和追踪裁判的轮转** 当球移动到弱侧，前导裁判迅速开始轮转。同时追踪裁判移动到中央裁判的位置。

   第二阶段 a：前导裁判的轮转——暂停 当球移动到弱侧，前导裁判应分析是否有弱侧快速投篮或突破的可能。这一秒（"一口气"）延迟称为暂停。如果一个队员投篮或是突破上篮就不必发动轮转，而中央裁判需要观察弱侧的情况。为什么呢？因为距离和静立原则需要被重视。

   第二阶段 b：前导裁判的轮转——观察限制区 前导裁判在轮转时应该迅速地走直线，同时还要时刻保持积极性。如果在限制区内有队员，那么这是前导裁判的主要责任对象。如果没有，前导裁判要在新的强侧寻找下一对有矛盾的对位或者有可能进入限制区的队员。

图 16：
球移动到中轴线，前导裁判移动到轮转发动点，中央裁判准备将视线移动到球上

图 17：
球移动到弱侧，前导裁判轮转并观察限制区或最近的一对对位

   第二阶段 c：追踪裁判轮转到中央裁判的位置 一旦追踪裁判确认中央裁判在弱侧接管了对球的监控之后，追踪裁判就应该把视线从球上移走，在轮转之前接管新的弱侧区域。研究表明，这是轮转的过程中最薄弱的环节之一，因为通常情况下追踪裁判的视线是锁定在球上的，而不是立即重新开始观察弱侧的矛盾。

Diagram 18:
When Centre has picked-up the ball, Trail shall pick-up the new weak side post play asap.

d. **Phase 2d: Rotation "not completed" by Lead** When Leads uses the proper technique to rotate (early start, walking sharply), Lead will be able to stop the rotation any time and return back to the initial position. The most common situations are drive/shot from the weak side during the rotation or skip pass to the other side of the court. When this occurs, the Centre does not move anywhere yet and will stay in Centre position. The Trail will return back to the initial position as Trail. As a principle, if Lead has passed the middle point of the backboard or the paint, the rotation should be completed as this is the point of no return.

Diagram 19:
Drive/shot from the weakside and Lead is able to abort and return back to referee.

Diagram 20:
Skip pass to the other side, Lead is able to stop and return back to the ballside.

图 18：
当中央裁判接管了对球的监控，追踪裁判需尽快接管对弱侧低位的监控

第二阶段 d：前导裁判未完成轮转 当前导裁判用恰当的技巧进行轮转时（早发动、快移动），他能随时停止轮转并回到其初始位置，最常见的情况是在轮转的过程中出现弱侧的突破、投篮或吊传到球场的另一侧。当这些发生时，中央裁判不要移动，应保持住其中央裁判的位置。追踪裁判回到其初始的追踪位置。原则上，如果前导裁判已经越过了篮板或限制区的中轴线，他应该继续完成轮转，因为已经跨过了返回的临界点了。

图 19：
弱侧的突破或投篮，前导裁判可以终止轮转并返回原点

图 20：
吊传至另一侧，前导裁判可以停止轮转并返回球侧

3. **Phase 3: Lead arrives to the ball side and Centre rotates to new Trail position**

   After Lead has completed the rotation, Centre is the last person to rotate to the new Trail position.

   a. **Phase 3a: Coverage by Centre & Lead** Centre will stay in centre position and referee the ball and any play around it until Lead has completed the rotation, is ready to referee the play, and the play is no longer active. If the play is progressing during the Lead rotation, Centre will stay with the play until it is completed and no longer active, before rotating to Trail. Our primary target is to continue to referee any play and then to move to the new position (rotate). As a result, there will always be two Centres momentarily.

   b. **Phase 3b: Rotation by Centre to the Trail position** When Centre moves up to the Trail position, this movement should be backwards and facing the basket at all times (45°).

Diagram 21:
C will stay with the play until L has completed the rotation and is ready to referee.

Diagram 22:
Old C is always the last one to move to the new T position (moving backwards) and now the rotation is completed.

4. **Misbalance – "partners do not pick-up" the rotation** While it should be avoided, there will be times when not all of the referees will be aware that there is a rotation in progress, and then a change in the direction of play occurs. Where this occurs, the referees should not panic as there are two options to adjust properly during a breakdown in the rotation while in transition. Normally, there is always at least one referee (but usually two), who is (are) aware of the situation.

3. **第三阶段：前导裁判移动到球侧，中央裁判轮转到新的追踪位置**
   在前导裁判完成了他的轮转之后，中央裁判移动到新的追踪位置，成为最后一个完成轮转的人。

   第三阶段 a：前导裁判和中央裁判覆盖的区域 中央裁判保持原来位置继续观察场上的有球区域，一直持续到前导裁判完成轮转并进入新的监控区域，且比赛不再活跃时。如果前导裁判在轮转过程中，有球区域的比赛十分激烈，那么中央裁判应当保持位置继续监控。我们首要的目标是要保证对比赛的监控，然后再移动到相应的位置。这样做的结果，会使场上暂时性地出现两名中央裁判。

   第三阶段 b：中央裁判移动到追踪裁判的位置 当中央裁判移动追踪的位置时，应向后移动，并且始终面向球篮（45°）。

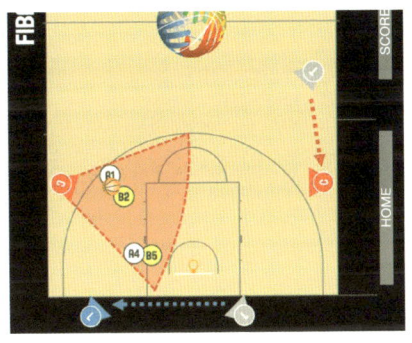

图 21：
C 保持对比赛的监管，直到 L 完成轮转并接管比赛

图 22：
原来的 C 永远是最后一个移动（后撤）到新 T 位置，此时轮转完成

第四阶段：失衡情况——"同伴没有接上"轮转 这应该是可以避免的，很多时候并不是所有的裁判员都能意识到轮转已经发动，然后突然发生攻防转换。当这种情况发生时，裁判员不必惊慌，因为在攻防转换发生失误时，有两种选择来进行适当调整。通常情况下，至少有一名裁判员（但通常是两名裁判员）会意识到这种情况。

a. **Option 1: New Lead & Centre** should always look for their partners and court balance while in transition. Identify what side the new Trail is on in the backcourt, and adjust accordingly in order to have correct balance when arriving in the frontcourt. You can use your voice or pre-designated signals amongst the crew to draw the attention of the referee who has missed the initial rotation.

b. **Option 2: New Trail** is always the last chance to balance the court coverage during a missed rotation in transition. Normally the new Trail has more time and an ideal view to see the progress of the transition play. If necessary, new Trail can move to the other side of the court during transition to have Trail and Lead on the same side. However, this should happen in the backcourt.

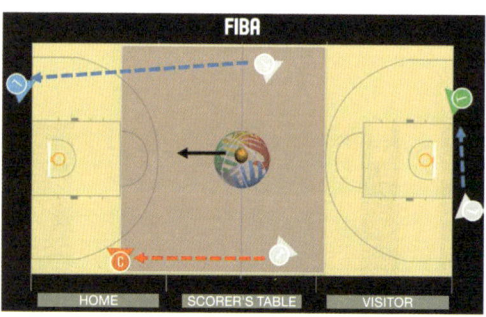

Diagram 23:
New C & L should always control the court in transition, before they arrive at the free throw line extended on the frontcourt.

Diagram 24:
Second option is that new T balances the court coverage by crossing the court diagonally, on the backcourt.

a. **选择 1：新的前导裁判和中央裁判**　应该在攻防转换时寻找同伴以及球场上的平衡。确定新的追踪裁判位于后场的哪一侧，之后据此进行调整，使得三人在到达前场时达到新的平衡。你可以使用声音或适当的信号来引起没有及时轮转到位置的裁判员的注意。

b. **选择 2：新的追踪裁判**　是在轮转发生失误时进行纠正以达到平衡的最后机会。通常情况下，新的追踪裁判有更多的时间和理想的视野来观察转换的进程。如有必要，新的追踪裁判可以移动到球场的任意一侧，以使追踪裁判和前导裁判处于相同的一侧。然而这必须在后场完成纠正。

图 23：
在转换中，新的 C 和 L 应该在到达前场的罚球线延长线之前持续监控比赛

图 24：
第二个选择是新的 T 可以通过在后场穿插到另一侧来保持场上的位置平衡

2.9 LEAD POSITION & TRANSITION

Target: To identify proper working area and coverage in the Lead positon.

During transition, the new Lead should be ahead of the play and arrive to the baseline in four seconds or less, and should be in a position ready to referee. The new Lead should also be in good position to referee the play throughout transition down the floor. This is only possible when the following correct techniques are applied:

a. Stay with the previous play before the new transition – namely, wait until the ball has entered the basket in the case of a successful shot for goal or when a defensive player has gained control of a rebound;

b. After turning with a power step, be sure to face the court all the time (when done properly, the referee should also able to pick-up the game clock);

c. Start transition with full speed and maintain it until arriving at the baseline;

d. Face the court during the entire transition (actively looking for next play to come and refereeing the defence);

e. Run straight to the baseline to set-up position (keeping same distance from the play all the way) – "out-side/out-side" angle;

f. Stop on the baseline with "one-two" count in a stationary position, and be ready to referee the play when it starts.

Diagram 25:
L moves correctly with straight line to the endline maintaining the same distance from the play – speed and size of the players remains same from the start to the end.

2.9 前导裁判的位置和攻防转换

目标：明确前导裁判的工作区域和视野覆盖。

在攻防转换中，新的前导裁判一般要在 4 秒之内移动到对面端线，并做好执裁准备，前导裁判在移动过程中也要保证有好的位置来执裁。下列技巧是能否良好宣判的重要所在：

a. 完全结束上一比赛片段后再转换位置，也就是说，要等投篮的球完全进入球篮或防守队获得篮板球；

b. 在转身用力蹬地跑向端线后，保持面向球场（当正确完成后，还应该保持对比赛计时钟的监控）；

c. 全速启动并保持速度直到到达端线；

d. 在整个转换过程中要面对球场（动态的观察接下来的比赛和执裁防守）；

e. 直线跑到端线位置并建立初始位置（保持与比赛的固定距离）——保持开角；

f. 停在端线的一个静立位置并默数"一、二"，并准备再次执裁接下来的比赛。

图 25：
L 正确地沿直线跑动，抵达端线并与比赛保持适当的距离——队员的速度和体型自始至终保持一致

Diagram 26:
L curves incorrectly close to the basket and the play is coming at L. The angle changes completely because players look bigger and faster.

Lead works on the baseline on a 45° angle facing the basket. Position should be not more than 1 metre from the baseline and normally outside the paint. The Lead's working area is from three-point line to the edge of the backboard.

The normal set-up point for Lead is between the lane line of the key, and the three-point line. The Lead should move on the baseline according to the movement of the ball, ensuring they have position on the edge of the play. The Lead should work off-the court.

The Lead should normally make all violation/foul calls on the strong side of the court below free-throw line. Studies have proved that when the Lead makes calls on the weak side (other side of the court), especially on a drive (high contact), the decisions are incorrect, and in many cases, fantasy calls occur with guessing (foul called where contact was legal or no contact at all). This type of call is called "Lead cross call" and should not happen. The Lead must trust that the Centre will make the call if there is illegal contact (trusting Lead & active Centre). On weak side drives Lead may call low and front swipes and illegal hand contacts from Leads side and which Centre is unable to see. Lead must have an open angle to make the call.

图 26：
L 错误地以曲线跑向球篮，使得比赛朝 L 而来。由于队员看起来更大更快，导致视角完全变化

前导裁判在端线执裁时应以 45° 斜对球篮站位。距离端线不应超过 1 米，并且通常在限制区之外。前导裁判的工作区应当从 3 分线到篮板的边缘位置。

前导裁判的初始位置位于 3 分线与限制区边线之间。前导裁判根据球的位置在端线上移动，确保一直处于比赛的边缘。前导裁判应在球场外执裁。

前导裁判应当判罚出位于强侧罚球线以下的所有违例和犯规。研究证明，当前导裁判吹罚弱侧时（场地的另一侧），尤其是针对持球突破（高位的接触），决定一般都是错的，在很多案例中，都是伴随着猜测的猜判，吹罚的犯规都是合法接触或根本没有接触，这被称为"前导裁判的跨区交叉宣判"。前导裁判必须相信，如果那些位置发生非法接触，中央裁判将会做出判罚（信任的前导裁判和积极的中央裁判）。对于弱侧的突破，前导裁判可以对低位的、前侧的击打以及前导裁判一侧的非法手部接触进行判罚，而这些动作，中央裁判是无法看到的。前导裁判有很好的开角来做出判罚。

FIBA REFEREES MANUAL

Diagram 27:
Lead working area is between 3 point line and edge of the board. To find out if you have the correct position is to check that you will see the front of the rim.

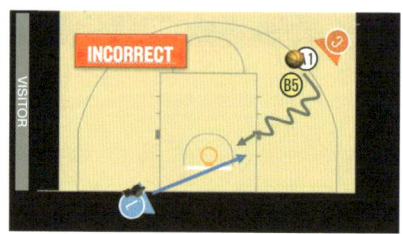

Diagram 28:
Lead must trust to the Centre who has to be active and ready cover his/her primary. The diagram demonstrates the "cross call" by Lead what is incorrect.

When ball comes to the strong side post (Lead's side) lead should prepare for a possible drive to the basket by taking few steps wider. This is called "Lead cross step". This allows Lead to see a possible drive to the basket, identify the possible help defence from the weak side, and implement the same "Distance & Stationary" principle as in transition.

Diagram 29:
When ball comes to the strong side low post, Lead prepares for the next play and by taking cross steps to have wider angle covering the next possible play.

Diagram 30:
L has taken the cross steps and turned slightly towards the basket. This new angle allows to referee the defence in the drive and prepare for the help defense.

图 27：
前导裁判的工作区位于 3 分线和篮板的边缘位置。想判断你是否处于正确的位置，就检查你是否看得到篮圈的前沿

图 28：
前导裁判必须相信中央裁判的积极性，以及对其主区的监控。图中显示了前导裁判错误的"跨区交叉宣判"

当球来到强侧的低位（前导裁判一侧），前导裁判应该移动几步，取得更开阔的视角以做好对可能出现的突破上篮的监控，这被称为"前导裁判的交叉步"。这使得前导裁判能更清楚地对突破上篮进行监控，并看到从弱侧过来的协防，在移动过程中同样要贯彻"距离与静立"原则。

图 29：
当球来到强侧的低位时，前导裁判应准备观察对抗，并使用前导交叉步，取得更开阔的角度，以便监控到下一个对抗的整体

图 30：
L 使用交叉步并向球篮轻微转动躯干。这个新的角度使得前导裁判能很好地监控到突破中的防守动作以及可能出现的协防

2.10 TRAIL POSITION & TRANSITION

Target: To identify proper working area and coverage in the Trail position

During transition, the new Trail should always trail the play (behind the play – not in line or in front of the play). This way the Trail is able to easily control the clocks and analyse the next possible plays to come. This is only possible when the following correct techniques are implemented:

a. Wait behind the baseline until the ball is either passed to a teammate on the court after a made basket and the thrower-in has advanced on to the court (the new Trail should wait to have a minimum of 3 meters distance from the ball before they step on to the court);

b. Always maintain a proper distance behind the play – 1-2 steps (no yo-yo running);

c. Be the last to arrive in the front court, and have a 45° angle facing the basket (all players should be between straight arms extended = right/left side sideline & left/right side centre line).

Diagram 31:
New T applies correct techniques by waiting behind the endline that ball is passed to the team mate after the basket and the thrower-in has advanced to the court.

Diagram 32:
T maintains the proper distance always behind the play (no yo-yo running) facilitating the steady wide angle and T is able to control the clocks and see the set-ups on the frontcourt.

2.10 追踪裁判的位置和攻防转换

目标：明确追踪裁判的工作区域和视野覆盖。

在攻防转换中，新的追踪裁判应该追踪比赛（始终位于比赛的后面——不要超越或平行于比赛）。这样追踪裁判可以轻松监控计时钟并分析下一次可能的对抗的到来。这些只有在应用正确的技术时才有可能实现：

a. 等在端线后边直到球中篮得分掷球入界的队员将球传给在球场上的队友，并且他自己也开始向前场推进（在进入场地之前，新的追踪裁判至少需要在球 3 米开外的距离等待）。

b. 总是保持在比赛后方 1~2 步的适当距离（不要折返跑）。

c. 最后一个进入前场，并保持面向球篮 45° 的站立位置（所有队员应在伸直的两臂延长线之间 = 右侧 / 左侧的边线和左侧 / 右侧的中线之间）。

图 31：
新的 T 采用了正确的技术，在球中篮后等在端线后边，直到掷球入界的队员将球传给队友，然后开始向前场移动

图 32：
T 一直位于比赛的后方（不要折返跑移动），并保持适当距离以维持固定的开角，并且他能监控计时钟和观察到前场的设置

Trail working area is between team bench area line and centre line. The Trail should be able to control a wide area if they are keeping a proper distance from the players with an active mind-set to analyse the next movements of the players. Trail normally works on the court.

When the ball moves closer to the Trail's sideline, Trail should move further into the court to maintain the open angle. Whenever a dribbler is positioned in front of Trail, the Trail should be assessing which direction the dribbler will move next. Whenever a player moves in one direction, the Trail should move to the other direction - this is called "Trail Cross Step". When the play is over, the Trail should return closer to the sideline in the standard working position.

Diagram 33:
Trail working area is between team bench area line and centre line. If ball moves to close to strong side sideline, T should take one-two steps on the court to maintain wide angle.

Diagram 34:
Whenever T is straight-lined, assess which side the player will move next. When player moves T should react and take cross step to the opposite direction of the players.

追踪裁判的工作区域位于球队席的边线和中线之间。如果追踪裁判与队员保持适当距离，并且预判队员要做的下一个动作，那么就可以监控较大的区域范围。追踪裁判一般在球场内执裁。

如果球朝追踪裁判所在的边线移动，他应该向场内移动，并保持开角。无论何时，追踪裁判都应当使运球队员位于他的前方，这样他可以主动判断运球队员要向哪个方向前进。当队员向某一方向运动时，追踪裁判应当向相反的方向运动，这被称为"追踪裁判的交叉步"。当对抗结束时，追踪裁判应当回到靠近边线的初始位置。

图 33：
追踪裁判的工作区位于球队席的边线与中线之间。如果球向 T 所在的边线移动时，他应当向场内移动一步到两步以保持开阔的视角

图 34：
当 T 处于闭角时，他需要预判队员下一步的移动方向。当队员移动时，T 必须使用交叉步，向相反的方向移动

45

2.11 CENTRE POSITION & TRANSITION

Target: To identify proper working area and coverage in the Centre positon

During the transition from Centre to Centre, the referee in question has to follow these techniques:

   a. Stay with the previous play before the new transition. Namely, wait until the ball has entered the basket in the case of a successful attempt for goal, or until a defensive player has gained control of a rebound;

   b. Face the court during the entire transition (actively looking for next play to come and refereeing defence);

   c. Run straight to the frontcourt free throw line extended (set-up position);

   d. When a transition play is advancing on the weak side, Centre might need to stop momentarily and referee the play (keep distance from the play – anticipate).

Centre working area is between top of the free throw circle and the imaginary "bottom of the free throw line circle". Practically speaking, this means the free throw line extended, a couple steps up, a couple steps down. The Centre working area is normally always on the court.

Any play on the weak side towards the basket is the Centre's primary. The Centre has to remember to be ready to make the call when there is illegal contact or action. If the Centre misses the illegal contact and is passive, this will force the Lead to be more active and in the worst case scenario, will result in "Lead cross calls" (trusting Lead & active Centre).

2.11 中央裁判的位置和攻防转换

目标：明确中央裁判的工作区域和视野覆盖。

从中央裁判转换到中央裁判的过程中，应当运用如下技巧：

a. 完全结束上一比赛片段后再转换位置——名义上，要等投篮的球完全进入球篮或防守队获得篮板球；

b. 转换的过程中全程面向场地（积极观察比赛的发展和执裁防守）；

c. 直线跑到前场罚球线延长线的位置（初始位置）；

d. 如果比赛在转换过程中发展到弱侧，那么中央裁判要立即停止移动，准备判罚（通过预判保持与比赛的合适距离）。

中央裁判的工作区位于罚球半圆的顶部和假想的罚球半圆底部之间。中央裁判的工作区，通常总是位于场地内。

任何弱侧向球篮发展的对抗都是由中央裁判负责，因此中央裁判必须谨记，要时刻准备好对非法接触或动作的吹罚。如果中央裁判对非法接触漏判或消极对待，那会迫使前导裁判承担更大压力，甚至会出现"前导跨区宣判"（信任的前导裁判和积极的中央裁判）。

Diagram 35:
Centre normally moves in the transition from backcourt to frontcourt free throw line extended facing court covering possible any weak side transition.

Diagram 36:
Centre's set-up position is at free throw line extended and working area from top of the free throw circle to the imaginary bottom of the free throw circle.

When there is a weak side drive to the basket, the Centre should take a step(s) on the court diagonally towards the centre line, or the same principle as with the Trail. Whenever a player moves in one direction, the Centre should move in the other direction. This is called "Centre cross step". There will always be a moment when the C is straight lined at the start of the drive, but this is only momentary and is minimized with the cross step.

Diagram 37:
Ball on the weak side and C prepares to referee the drive to the basket (mentally ready to take cross step).

Diagram 38:
Dribbler moved to the left and C correctly cross step(s) to the right and maintains the open angle.

图 35：
中央裁判通常的移动位置是从后场到前场罚球线延长线的位置，应当面向场地监控所有弱侧的攻防转换

图 36：
中央裁判的初始位置位于罚球线延长线，工作区域位于罚球半圆的顶部和假想的罚球半圆底部之间

当弱侧出现突破上篮，中央裁判需要向场内中线方向斜向移动几步，或者与追踪裁判使用相同的原则。当一名队员向某一方向移动时，中央裁判需要向相反的方向移动，这被称为"中央裁判的交叉步"。有些时候中央裁判位于突破发起的闭角位置，但这只是瞬间的并且用交叉步就可以化解。

图 37：
球在弱侧，中央裁判做好执裁突破上篮的准备（思想上准备好进行交叉步）

图 38：
运球队员向左侧移动，中央裁判正确使用交叉步移动到其右侧并保持开角

49

In case of trap situation in the frontcourt on the weak side and close to the centre line, C moves closer to the centre line to referee the play ("go wherever you need to referee the play"). After the trap situation is over Centre will return to the normal position at the free throw line extended, unless Lead has rotated during the trap (although should have rotated before the trap).

Diagram 39:
When there is a trap close to the centre line on the weak side of the court C needs to move closer to the centre line in order to cover the play properly, but this is not rotation (unless L is rotating).

Diagram 40:
After the trap is over C will return to initial position and working area at the free throw line extended (unless L has rotated during the trap – first option).

当出现弱侧的靠近中线位置的包夹情况时，中央裁判应当靠近中线以观察比赛（"去你需要的地方以监控比赛"）。包夹结束后，中央裁判返回罚球线延长线的常规位置，除非在包夹发生时，前导已经发动了轮转（本应该可以在之前就发动轮转）。

图 39：
当靠近弱侧中线出现包夹情况时，中央裁判需要移动靠近中线位置以监控比赛，但这不是轮转（除非 L 轮转）

图 40：
当包夹结束时，中央裁判应当返回罚球线延长线的常规位置（除非包夹发生时，L 已经发动了轮转——第一选择）

2.12 FAST BREAK

Target: To identify proper coverage and Lead-Centre cooperation during a fast break

During the fast break, it is important to understand that the Centre has to be active and has 50% of the coverage (weak side).

Any action or contact on the weak side should be covered by Centre, and any action on the strong side by Lead. This is the beauty of 3PO when it works properly.

It is good to practise when running from Trail to Lead in transition to automatically identify where the Centre is on the other side of the court. When this becomes a standard procedure, it will also automatically happen during the fast break when time is more limited.

The Lead and Centre need to run at full speed, analyse when the play will start, and then stop and referee the play by focusing on the defence (referee defence). The weak point in coverage during the fast break is when the new Lead curves under the basket and tries to referee the action on the weak side. This destroys the concept of 3PO as each referee is responsible for their own primary and there should be no need for secondary.

It is important that the Centre quickly arrives in the front court at the free throw line extended to have the best coverage for a possible basket interference or goaltending (see also *"2.20 Basket interference & goaltending"* for more details).

Diagram 41:
C has to run fast in every fast break. It is important that both L & C are able to have a stationary position to referee when the play starts. This is normally a dual coverage situation.

2.12 快攻

目标：明确快攻中适当的区域分工以及前导—中央裁判的配合。

在快攻中，明确中央裁判应该积极主动并且负责 50% 的区域分工（弱侧）。

任何弱侧的动作与接触都应由中央裁判观察，同时强侧的动作应由前导裁判负责。这就是正确运行 3 人执裁的精彩之处。

由追踪裁判变为前导裁判的转换过程中，能去自然感觉到中央裁判在场地另一侧的位置是需要勤于练习的，因为这需要成为一种标准的程序，即使当时间有限的快攻发生时，也能自然而然地形成。

追踪裁判和前导裁判需要全速奔跑，分析动作开始的时机，而后停下通过注意防守来观察动作（执裁防守）。在快攻的区域分工中切忌新的前导裁判切入篮下试图去观察弱侧的动作，这打破了 3 人执裁的概念，即每名裁判员应负责各自的主要责任区，而并非监控次要责任区。

中央裁判应当快速跑到前场的罚球线延长线，寻找最好的角度视野去观察可能出现的干扰得分或干涉得分（详细参见"2.20 干扰得分和干涉得分"）。

图 41：
C 在快攻中必须全力奔跑，L 和 C 在快攻中静立宣判十分重要，通常情况下快攻是两名裁判共同覆盖的

2.13 PRESS DEFENCE

Target: To identify proper coverage and Trail-Centre cooperation during a press .

When there is more than two opponent pair of players in the backcourt the Centre has to be active and help Trail to cover the play. If all the players are in the backcourt also the Lead has to adjust their position closer to the play ready to cover any potential long passes.

All players in the backcourt

Diagram 42:
T and C referee the action in the backcourt.

More than 4 opponent players in the backcourt

Diagram 43:
T referees behind the play. C takes a position close to centre line to referee players in front or backcourt. L takes position on the endline to referee players in frontcourt.

2.13 紧逼防守

目标：明确紧逼时适当的区域分工以及追踪—中央裁判的配合。

当后场出现两对以上的攻防矛盾时，中央裁判必须积极观察并协助追踪裁判监控比赛。如果所有队员都在后场，那么前导裁判也需要调整他的位置，靠近比赛以便监控可能出现的长传。

所有队员都在后场

图 42：
T 和 C 执裁后场的比赛情况

超过四名对方队员在后场

图 43：
T 在比赛后方执裁，C 占据靠近中线的位置并监控在前场或后场的队员，L 占据前场端线的位置并监控前场的队员

2.14 OUT-OF-BOUNDS & THROW-INS

Target: To understand coverage on out-of-bounds plays to ensure that only one referee always makes the "out-of-bounds" call.

3PO covers all of the boundary lines in the frontcourt. Only the Trail has two lines to cover. The basic rule is that Lead covers the baseline, Centre covers the weak side sideline, and Trail covers the strong side sideline and centre line.

When the game continues with a throw-in there should always be two referees (Lead & Trail) on the side of a throw-in.

Diagram 44:
L & C has one boundary line to cover, while T has two lines (sideline and centreline).

Diagram 45: When the throw-in is on the frontcourt's endline between 3 point line and edge of the backboard, L's position is outside of the throw-in spot (C has to be ready to cover weak side). T mirrors the "time-in" signal to the table.

Diagram 46: When the throw-in is on the frontcourt's endline between 3 point line and sideline, L's position is between basket and throw-in spot. T mirrors the "time-in" signal to the table.

2.14 球出界与掷球入界

目标：理解球出界情况下的区域分工以及明确只应有一名裁判员做出"球出界"的宣判。

3人执裁的观察范围覆盖了前场的所有界线。只有追踪裁判负责观察两条线。其基本原则为：前导裁判负责端线，中央裁判负责弱侧的边线，同时追踪裁判负责强侧的边线和中线。

当掷球入界恢复比赛时，掷球入界一侧总有两名裁判员（前导裁判和追踪裁判）。

图44：
L和C各负责一条界线，T负责两条界线（边线和中线）

图45：
当掷球入界地点位于前场3分线与篮板边界之间的端线处，L的位置在掷球入界点的外侧（C准备观察弱侧）。T向记录台做出镜像的"开动计时钟"的手势

图46：
当掷球入界地点位于前场3分线与边线之间的端线处，L的位置在球篮与掷球入界点之间。T向记录台做出镜像的"开动计时钟"的手势

2.15 SHOT COVERAGE (GENERAL & 3 POINTS ATTEMPTS)

Target: To identify and understand the coverage of each referee during shots for goal.

The basic principle is that the Lead has primary coverage on any 2 point shots on the strong side (as demonstrated below, blue area) and the Trail has primary coverage for all 3 point shots, and 2 point shots on the strong side.

The Centre has primary coverage on all shots on the weak side (see Diagram 47).

Whenever there is dual coverage (restricted area, rectangle 2), the basic principle is that the respective referee covers their side of the play (see Diagram 48).

See also *"2.11 Covering a shot (protect the shooter)"*, *"2.3 Refereeing the defence"* & *"2.4 Stay with the play"* in FIBA Referee Manual –Individual Officiating Techniques (IOT).

 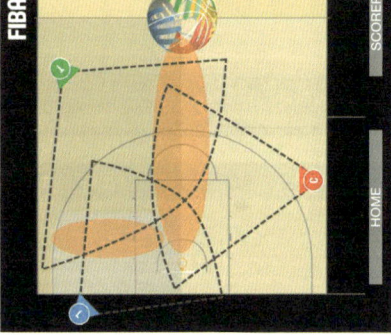

Diagram 47:
L has normally the primary coverage in blue area, T in green area and C in red area.

Diagram 48:
In dual coverage areas it is important that both referees have the discipline to process the entire play and try to focus only for their side of the defensive players.

2.15 投篮的区域分工（一般情况与 3 分试投）

目标：确认和理解在投篮情况下，每名裁判员的区域分工。

基本原则是前导裁判负责强侧的任何 2 分投篮（如下图蓝色区域所示），追踪裁判负责所有的 3 分投篮以及强侧的 2 分投篮。中央裁判负责弱侧的所有投篮。见图 47。

不管何时出现共管区（限制区，2 区），基本原则都是裁判员分别对各自的区域负主要责任。见图 48。

参考《国际篮联裁判员手册：个人执裁技术》中"2.11 观察一次投篮情况（保护投手）""2.3 执裁防守""2.4 观察比赛情况的始末。"

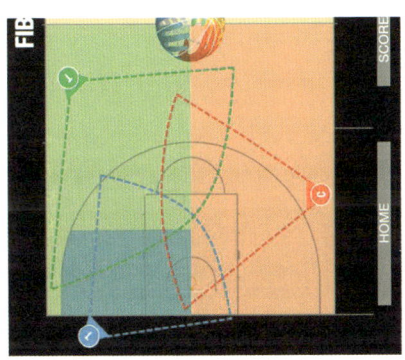

图 47：
通常 L 的主要责任区为蓝色区域，T 为绿色区域，C 为红色区域。

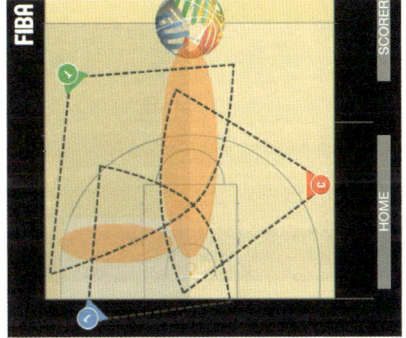

图 48：
在共管区域内，两名裁判员都有义务观察整个动作的发生并集中注意力在他们一侧的防守队员。

2.16 TIME-OUTS

After the table officials have notified the referees about the time-out request, normally the Trail or Centre closest to the table will signal the time-out.

Referees have three standard positions during the time-outs (always on the opposite side). They can select any of the three positions they feel are the most appropriate (Note: leave the ball on the court where the game will be resumed).

When a time-out has 20 seconds remaining, two referees will move close to the team bench areas in order to be ready to activate the teams to return back to the court when the 50 seconds warning signal sounds.

Diagram 49:
The three standard time-out positions, always in the opposite side.

Diagram 50:
When 20 seconds remaining of the time-out, two referees move close to the team bench areas.

2.16 暂停

在记录台人员将请求暂停的请求告知裁判后，通常由最靠近记录台的追踪裁判或中央裁判做出暂停信号。

在暂停期间，裁判员有三种标准的站位（总是在记录台对侧）。他们应选择他们感觉最适合的一种站位方法（注意：把球放置在比赛将要恢复的位置上）。

当暂停时间剩余 20 秒时，两名裁判员移动到球队席区附近，这是为了准备在 50 秒信号响起时提醒队员们做好准备回到场上。

图 49：
暂停时三名裁判标准的站立位置，位于对侧

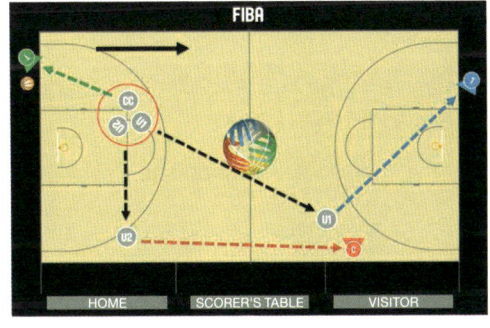

图 50：
当暂停还有 20 秒剩余时间，两名裁判员移动到靠近球队席区域的地方

Last 2:00 minutes (L2M) time-out protocol

(where a team has the opportunity to advance the ball to the frontcourt)

When the clock shows 2:00 minutes or less in the fourth quarter and in overtime when the team requesting the time-out is entitled to possession of the ball from its backcourt:

- Referees have three standard positions during the time-outs (always on the opposite side). They can select any of the three positions they feel are the most appropriate.

- During the time-out, the ball is to remain in the hands of the crew chief (this signals that a decision for the throw-in location is yet to be made).

- When a time-out has 20 seconds remaining, the crew chief and the one of the umpires will move close to the team bench areas. The crew chief will go to the team that is entitled to possession of the ball.

- When the 50 seconds signal sounds the officials will activate the teams to return back to the court.

- The crew chief will ask the head coach to decide whether the throw-in will remain in the backcourt or whether it will advance to the frontcourt. The crew chief will verbally confirm the decision with the Head Coach (e.g. "The throw-in will be in the back / front court."). The crew chief will show a signal to the location of the throw-in by pointing to and moving to that location for the throw-in. Verbal support of this will accompany the signal.

- The crew chief will normally administer the throw-in, with the other two referees adjusting their positions accordingly.

- The referees shall ensure that the shot clock is appropriately set (reset/remain) before the throw-in.

最后 2 分钟（L2M）暂停规定

（球队有机会决定在前场掷球入界）

在第 4 节和每一决胜期的比赛计时钟显示 2:00 分钟或更少时，在后场拥有球权的队请求了暂停：

- 在暂停期间，裁判员有三个标准的站立位置（位于对侧）。他们可以选择三个位置中任意一个最合适的。
- 在暂停期间，球应该在主裁判的手里（这表明了掷球入界的地点还没有确定）。
- 当暂停时间还剩 20 秒时，主裁判和一名助理裁判员将移动到球队席区域。主裁判移动到有掷球入界球权的球队。
- 当 50 秒信号响起时，裁判员提醒队员们回到比赛场地。
- 主裁判应询问主教练决定接下来的掷球入界是在后场比赛停止时的地点执行或是在前场执行。主裁判需要口语重复主教练的决定（例如"掷球入界要在后/前场执行"）。主裁判要用手势指明掷球入界的地点以及移动到该地点管理掷球入界。口语的提示要伴随着相应的手势。
- 通常由主裁判来管理这次掷球入界，其他两名裁判员相应调整各自的位置。
- 主裁判应确保在掷球入界前，设置正确的进攻计时钟时间（复位/保持）。

2.17 SUBSTITUTIONS

Trail or Centre closest to the table will administer the substitutions. All substitutions should be completed as quickly as possible. As soon as all substitutions are completed the administering referee should make sure there is a correct number of players on the playing court and shall then communicate by establishing eye contact with the active referee with the ball.

Substitutions after a foul call

After the calling referee has finished the reporting to the table it is the responsibility of the new table side referee (Trail or Centre) to administer substitutions.

Diagram 51:
T has finished reporting and moves to a new position for free throws. New C will then administer substitutions.

2.18 EIGHT SECONDS & BACKCOURT VIOLATIONS

Normally Trail has the primary responsibility to count the 8 seconds. On all press situations Centre should be ready to assist the Trail (physically and mentally engaged with the play).

Trail also has the primary responsibility on all centre line violations. Sometimes the Centre can also help with possible backcourt violations when the ball is played on the weak side before returning to the backcourt.

2.17 替换

最靠近记录台的追踪裁判或中央裁判要管理替换。所有替换应尽可能快地完成。在替换完成时，执行裁判应确认场上正确的队员数量随后应与负责管理球的裁判员建立眼神交流。

宣判一起犯规后的替换

在宣判犯规的裁判员完成向记录台的报告后，新的记录台侧的裁判员追踪裁判或中央裁判要负责管理替换。

图 51：
T 在完成报告犯规后移动到了新的位置准备罚球程序。新的 C 随后管理替换

2.18 8 秒违例与球回后场违例

通常来说追踪裁判对于 8 秒的计数负主要责任。在所有的紧逼情况时，中央裁判应随时准备去协助追踪裁判（身体和精神都要融入比赛）。

追踪裁判同样对所有的球回后场违例负主要责任。有时当球在弱侧回场之前时，中央裁判同样可以协助可能的球回后场违例。

2.19 SHOT CLOCK COVERAGE

Normally it is the outside referees (Trail and Centre) who have primary responsibility for shot clock violations. Also the Lead should be aware of the time on the shot clock and to be ready to assist Trail / Centre in their decisions. It is vital for referees to know when the shot clock period is nearing its end to be able to make correct decisions in shot clock situations.

At all times the active referee administering the throw-in should check the shot clock to be sure it is set correctly. This must be done before referee passes the ball to the thrower-in.

Note: When the backboard is equipped with yellow lighting along its perimeter at the top, the lighting takes precedence over the shot clock signal sound.

2.20 BASKET INTERFERENCE & GOALTENDING

Normally the Trail or Centre referee is responsible to determine if a basket interference or goaltending violation occurs. The referee opposite the shot has the primary responsibility for the flight of the ball and goaltending / basket interference violations. See also Diagram 93 & Diagram 94.

If a basket is awarded due to basket interference or goaltending the calling referee shall stop the clock and count the goal by showing the correct official signal.

Basket interference & goaltending on a fast break

In fast break situations it is primarily Centre's and secondarily Lead's responsibility to cover the possible basket interference or goaltending violation. If the Centre is not ready to cover (physically not engaged with the play) the fast break it becomes Lead's responsibility. In this case the Lead should stop ahead of the endline to be able to see the ring and front of the backboard.

2.19 进攻计时钟的区域分工

通常外侧的裁判员（追踪裁判和中央裁判）对进攻时间违例负主要责任。同时前导裁判也应注意进攻计时钟上的时间以便于随时协助追踪裁判/中央裁判的判罚。裁判员了解什么时候进攻周期临近结束并随之做出正确的进攻时间违例的判罚是至关重要的。

所有情况下，管理掷球入界的执行裁判应检查进攻计时钟是否显示正确的时间，并且需在将球交于掷球入界队员前完成此程序。

注意：当篮板上沿装有黄色光带时，光带信号亮先于进攻计时钟信号响。

2.20 干扰得分和干涉得分

通常追踪裁判或中央裁判负责判罚是否发生一起干扰得分或干涉得分。投篮对侧的裁判员要对球的飞行以及干扰/干涉得分违例负主要责任。见图93与图94。

如果判给得分是因为干扰得分或干涉得分违例，宣判的裁判员应先停止比赛计时钟随后用官方的手势来表示应计得分有效。

一次快攻情况中的干扰得分与干涉得分

在快攻情况中，中央裁判对监控有可能出现的干涉得分或干扰得分违例负有主要责任，追踪裁判负有次要责任。如果中央裁判没有准备好去监控快攻（由于身体原因没有跟上比赛），那么这就变成前导裁判的责任了。在这种情况下，前导裁判应当停步在端线前，尽可能看到篮圈和篮板的正面。

Diagram 52:
Normally in fast break situations Centre is responsible for basket interference or goaltending violations.

Diagram 53:
If Centre is not engaged with the fast break then it becomes Lead's responsibility to cover basket interference / goaltending violations. In this case the Lead should stop ahead of the endline to be able to see the ring and front of the backboard.

Basket interference & goaltending on a foul play

On all plays resulting in a foul call the Trail and Centre should not relax after the call. Instead they should hold their position, maintain their focus and follow the situation until the end (when the ball no longer has possibility to enter the basket) and be ready to make possible BI / GT call.

图52：
在快攻情况中，通常中央裁判对发生干扰得分或干涉得分违例负责

图53：
若中央裁判没有跟上快攻，前导裁判将要观察并对干扰得分／干涉得分违例负责。在这种情况下前导裁判应当停步在端线前尽可能看到篮圈和篮板的正面

犯规中的干涉得分和干扰得分违例

在裁判员吹罚了犯规之后，追踪裁判和中央裁判不应该放松。相反应该在这起情况结束（当球不再有可能进入球篮）之前保持他们的位置和注意力，并做好准备宣判有可能出现的干涉得分或干扰得分违例。

2.21 REPORTING FOULS & SWITCHING

Target: To identify and know the correct positions and procedures after a foul is called.

Principle for the switches:

Free throws (ball remains in the frontcourt):

- a. Referee who reports the foul, moves to the opposite side in T position
- b. Other 2 fill up the empty spots

Throw-in (ball remains in the frontcourt):

- a. Referee who reports the foul, moves to the opposite side in T or C position
- b. Other 2 fill up the empty spots

Minimize distance – walk sharp – think where is your next position after reporting. If two referees call the same foul, the referee who is on the opposite side will report the foul.

In all situations referees should try to minimize switches. Sometimes there is no switching needed, sometimes all three referees need to move in order for the above rules to be implemented.

Reporting:

- a. Use clear voice
- b. Sharp signals
- c. Rhythm

See also *"2.8.1. Reporting"* in FIBA Referee Manual –Individual Officiating Techniques (IOT) for reporting technique and procedures.

2.21 报告犯规与换位

目标：明确和理解吹罚一起犯规后正确的落位与程序。

换位的原则：

罚球（球仍位于前场）

a. 向记录台报号的裁判，移动到记录台对侧追踪裁判的位置

b. 另外两名裁判员填补其余空位

掷球入界（球仍位于前场）

a. 向记录台报号的裁判，移动到记录台侧对追踪裁判或中央裁判的位置

b. 另外两名裁判填补其余空位

最短的距离—快步走—思考报号后移动的下一个位置。如果两名裁判员同时对一起犯规鸣哨，那么由位于记录台对侧的裁判员宣判这个犯规。

在所有情况下，裁判员应该尽量减少换位，为了实施以下的规则，有时裁判员无需换位，有时三名裁判都需要移动位置。

报告犯规：

a. 声音清楚洪亮

b. 手势简单有力

c. 节奏清晰明了

更多报告犯规的技术与程序参见《国际篮联裁判员手册：个人执裁技术》中"2.8.1 报告"。

Play remains in frontcourt, continued by throw-in

Diagram 54:
Call frontcourt table side by L – ball remains in the frontcourt (throw-in)

Diagram 55:
Call frontcourt table side by T – ball remains in the frontcourt (throw-in)

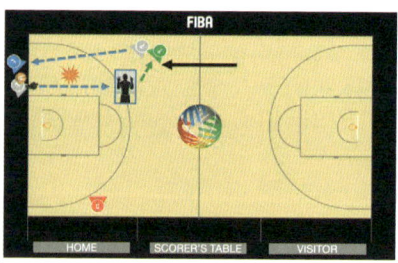

Diagram 56:
Call frontcourt opposite side by L – ball remains in the frontcourt (throw-in)

Diagram 57:
Call frontcourt opposite side by T – ball remains in the frontcourt (throw-in)

Diagram 58:
Call frontcourt table side by C – ball remains in the frontcourt (throw-in)

Diagram 59:
Call frontcourt opposite side by C – ball remains in the frontcourt (throw-in)

球仍留在前场，随后以掷球入界恢复比赛

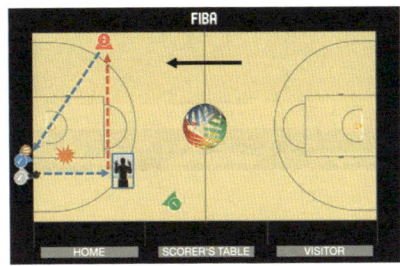

图 54：
前场记录台侧 L 鸣哨——球仍留在前场（掷球入界）

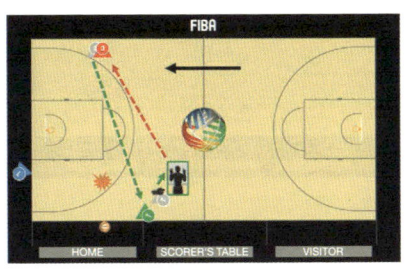

图 55：
前场记录台侧 T 鸣哨——球仍留在前场（掷球入界）

图 56：
前场对侧 L 鸣哨——球仍留在前场（掷球入界）

图 57：
前场对侧 T 鸣哨——球仍留在前场（掷球入界）

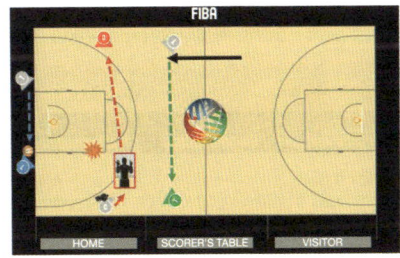

图 58：
记录台侧 C 鸣哨——球仍留在前场（掷球入界）

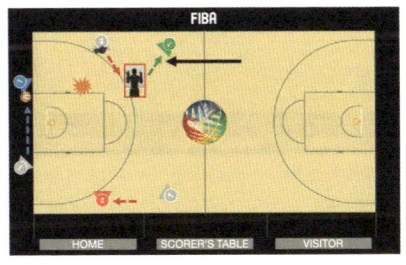

图 59：
前场对侧 C 鸣哨——球仍留在前场（掷球入界）

FIBA REFEREES MANUAL

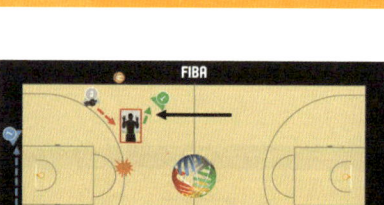

Diagram 60:
Double call frontcourt by T & C – ball remains in the frontcourt (throw-in)

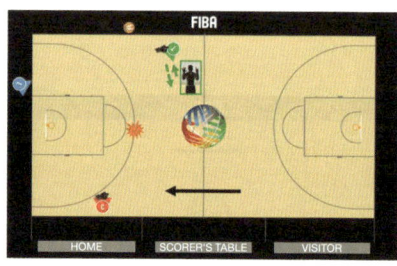

Diagram 61:
Double call frontcourt by T & C – ball remains in the frontcourt (throw-in)

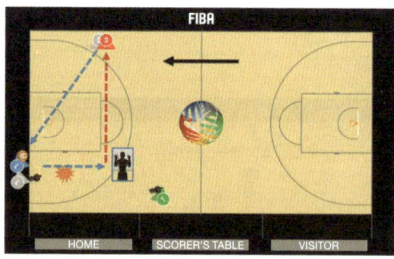

Diagram 62:
Double call frontcourt table side by T & L – ball remains in the frontcourt (throw-in)

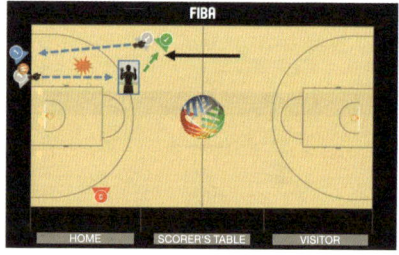

Diagram 63:
Double call frontcourt opposite side by T & L – ball remains in the frontcourt (throw-in)

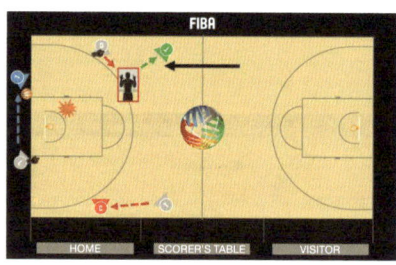

Diagram 64:
Double call frontcourt by L & C – ball remains in the frontcourt (throw-in)

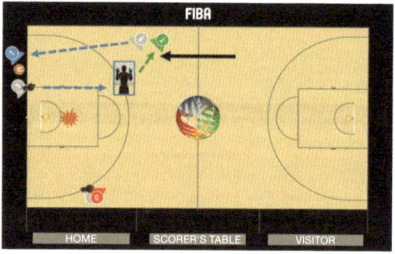

Diagram 65:
Double call frontcourt by L & C – ball remains in the frontcourt (throw-in)

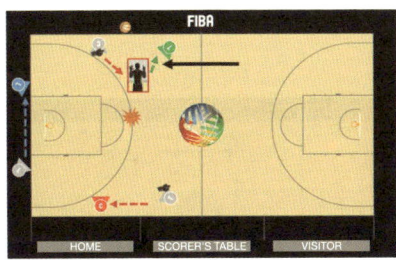

图 60：
前场 T 与 C 同时鸣哨——球仍留在前场（掷球入界）

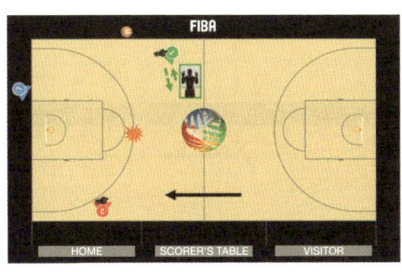

图 61：
前场 T 与 C 同时鸣哨——球仍留在前场（掷球入界）

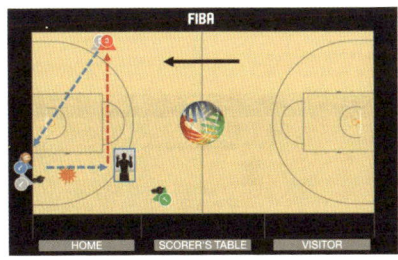

图 62：
前场记录台侧 T 与 L 同时鸣哨——球仍留在前场（掷球入界）

图 63：
前场对侧 T 与 L 同时鸣哨——球仍留在前场（掷球入界）

图 64：
前场 L 与 C 同时鸣哨——球仍留在前场（掷球入界）

图 65：
前场 L 与 C 同时鸣哨——球仍留在前场（掷球入界）

FIBA REFEREES MANUAL

Play remains in frontcourt, continued by free throw(s)

Diagram 66:
Call frontcourt table side by L – ball remains in the frontcourt (free throws)

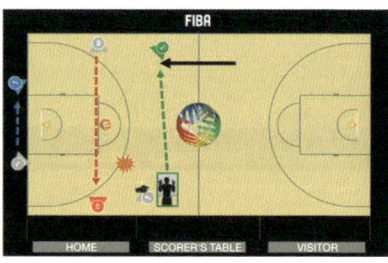

Diagram 67:
Call frontcourt table side by T – ball remains in the frontcourt (free throws)

Diagram 68:
Call frontcourt opposite side by L – ball remains frontcourt (free throws)

Diagram 69:
Call frontcourt opposite side by T – ball remains in the frontcourt (free throws)

Diagram 70:
Call frontcourt table side by C – ball remains in the frontcourt (free throws)

Diagram 71:
Call frontcourt opposite side by C – ball remains in the frontcourt (free throws)

球仍留在前场，随后以罚球恢复比赛

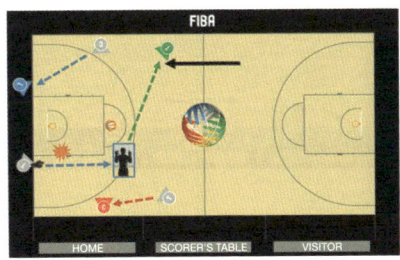

图 66：
前场记录台侧 L 鸣哨——球仍留在前场（罚球）

图 67：
前场记录台侧 T 鸣哨——球仍留在前场（罚球）

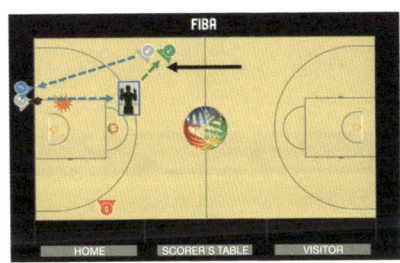

图 68：
前场对侧 L 鸣哨——球仍留在前场（罚球）

图 69：
前场对侧 T 鸣哨——球仍留在前场（罚球）

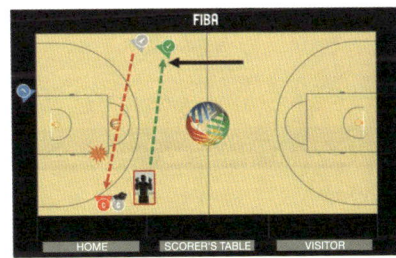

图 70：
前场记录台侧 C 鸣哨——球仍留在前场（罚球）

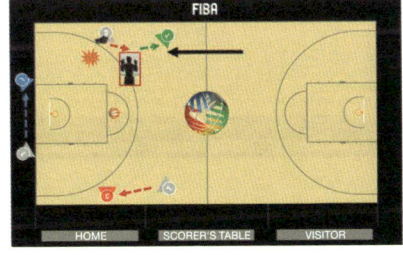

图 71：
前场对侧 C 鸣哨——球仍留在前场（罚球）

FIBA REFEREES MANUAL

Diagram 72:
Double call frontcourt by T & C – ball remains in the frontcourt (free throws)

Diagram 73:
Double call frontcourt by T & C – ball remains in the frontcourt (free throws)

Diagram 74:
Double call frontcourt table side by T & L – ball remains in the frontcourt (free throws)

Diagram 75:
Double call frontcourt opposite side by T & L – ball remains in the frontcourt (free throws)

Diagram 76:
Double call frontcourt by L & C – ball remains in the frontcourt (free throws)

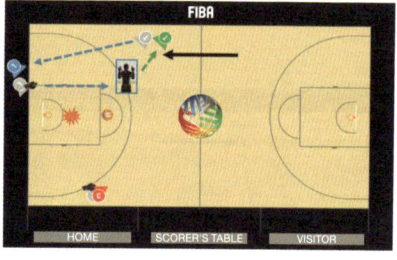

Diagram 77:
Double call frontcourt by L & C – ball remains in the frontcourt (free throws)

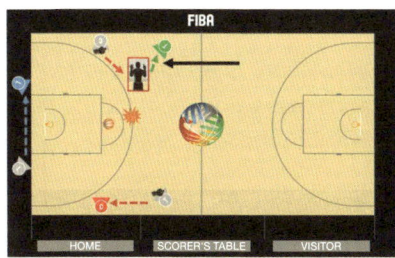

图 72：
前场 T 与 C 同时鸣哨——球仍留在前场
（罚球）

图 73：
前场 T 与 C 同时鸣哨——球仍留在前场
（罚球）

图 74：
前场记录台侧 T 与 L 同时鸣哨——球仍
留在前场（罚球）

图 75：
前场对侧 T 与 L 同时鸣哨——球仍留在前
场（罚球）

图 76：
前场 L 与 C 同时鸣哨——球仍留在前场
（罚球）

图 77：
前场 L 与 C 同时鸣哨——球仍留在前场
（罚球）

Play continues from new backcourt by throw-in

Note: When a foul is called in the backcourt or there is an offensive foul in the frontcourt, there is no switch unless it is necessary to facilitate the new position of the reporting referee on the opposite side (no long switches).

Diagram 78:
Call backcourt table side by L – ball moves new direction (throw-in)

Diagram 79:
Call backcourt opposite side by L – ball moves new direction (throw-in)

Diagram 80:
Call backcourt table side by T – ball moves new direction (throw-in)

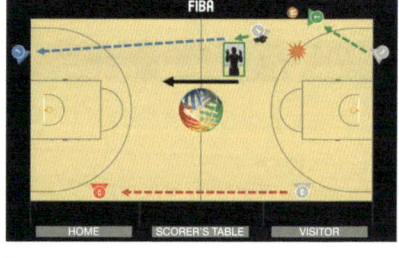

Diagram 81:
Call backcourt opposite side by T – ball moves new direction (throw-in)

Diagram 82:
Call backcourt table side by C – ball moves new direction (throw-in)

Diagram 83:
Call backcourt opposite side by C – ball moves new direction (throw-in)

在新的后场以掷球入界恢复比赛

注意：当在后场宣判一起犯规或在前场出现一起进攻犯规时，不需要轮转，除非需要为正在报告犯规的裁判员留出对侧新的位置（不要长距离转换位置）。

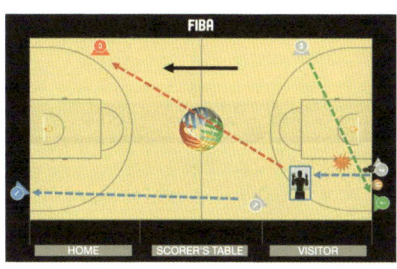

图 78：
后场记录台侧 L 鸣哨——球向新的方向发展（掷球入界）

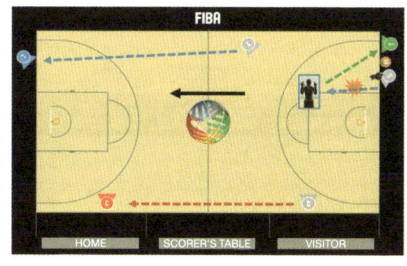

图 79：
后场对侧 L 鸣哨——球向新的方向发展（掷球入界）

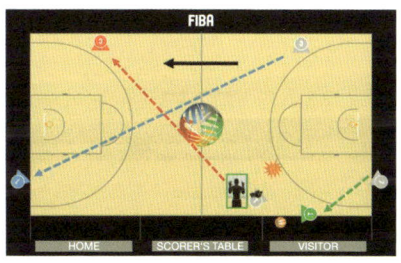

图 80：
后场记录台侧 T 鸣哨——球向新的方向发展（掷球入界）

图 81：
后场对侧 T 鸣哨——球向新的方向发展（掷球入界）

图 82：
后场记录台侧 C 鸣哨——球向新的方向发展（掷球入界）

图 83：
后场对侧 C 鸣哨——球向新的方向发展（掷球入界）

Play continues from the opposite end of the court by free throw(s)

Diagram 84:
Call backcourt table side by L – ball moves new direction (free thows)

Diagram 85:
Call backcourt opposite side by L – ball moves new direction (free thows)

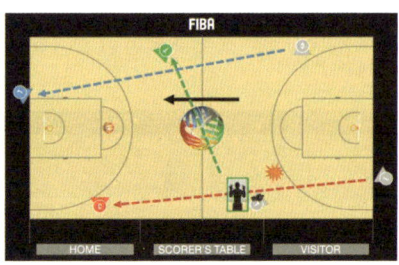

Diagram 86:
Call backcourt table side by T – ball moves new direction (free thows)

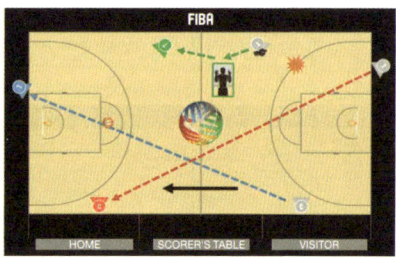

Diagram 87:
Call backcourt opposite side by T – ball moves new direction (free thows)

Diagram 88:
Call backcourt table side by C – ball moves new direction (free throws)

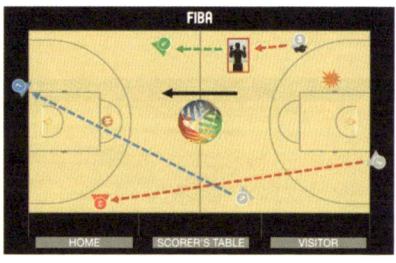

Diagram 89:
Call backcourt opposite side by C – ball moves new direction (free throws)

罚球后从对侧端线外恢复比赛

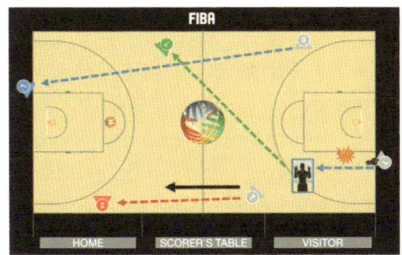

图 84：
后场记录台侧 L 鸣哨——球向新的方向发展（罚球）

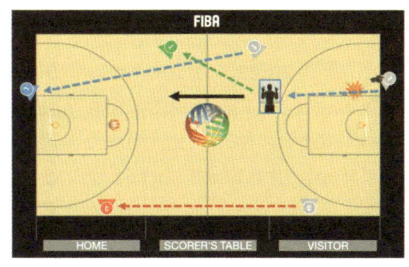

图 85：
后场对侧 L 鸣哨——球向新的方向发展（罚球）

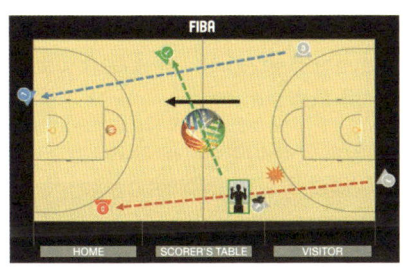

图 86：
后场记录台侧 T 鸣哨——球向新的方向发展（罚球）

图 87：
后场对侧 T 鸣哨——球向新的方向发展（罚球）

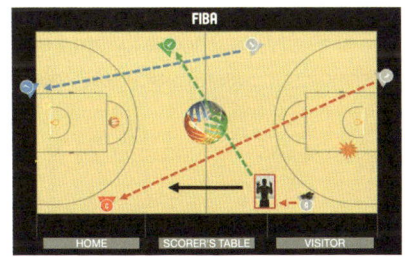

图 88：
后场记录台侧 C 鸣哨——球向新的方向发展（罚球）

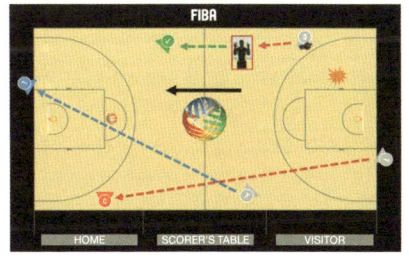

图 89：
后场对侧 C 鸣哨——球向新的方向发展（罚球）

2.22 FREE THROW COVERAGE

Target: To understand coverage and responsibilities during free throw situations and on following rebound plays.

In 3PO the Lead is the active referee in all free throw situations. Lead will administer all the free throws. During last free throw Lead is responsible for the players in rebound places on table side of the restricted area. For the last free-throw, the Lead should be positioned in the normal Lead set up position.

Centre indicates the number of free-throws using the official signals. On the all free throws, Centre is responsible of checking that there is no violation from the shooter. During last free throw Centre is responsible for the players in rebound places on opposite side of the restricted area. During the free-throws, the Centre is to be positioned near the side line in the normal Centre position.

Trail is responsible for the rest of the players behind the free-throw line extended and behind the 3-point line during all free throws.

When a violation occurs during the free throw and the ball is in the air, the referee should immediately blow the whistle to indicate the violation (exception: fake by free-throw shooter). This is to minimize any unnecessary escalation of p hysical contact between players after a violation occurs. There is no need to wait if the ball enters the basket or not.

If the ball enters the basket:

a. violation by free-throw shooter - basket is not valid.

b. violation by other players – basket is valid, whistle is to be ignored and play will continue with throw-in as after any successful last free-throw.

2.22 罚球的区域分工

目标: 理解罚球期间的视野覆盖和责任分工以及后续的篮板球情况。

3人执裁时前导裁判在所有的罚球情况中都是执行裁判。前导裁判要管理所有的罚球。在最后一次罚球中,前导裁判要负责观察位于记录台侧限制区边缘的分位区内的队员。对于最后一次罚球,前导裁判应位于通常情况下的初始位置。

中央裁判做出指示罚球次数的官方手势。所有的罚球情况中,中央裁判负责观察是否出现罚球队员的违例。中央裁判负责观察位于对侧限制区边缘的分位区内的队员。在罚球中,中央裁判应位于靠近边线处通常情况下的初始位置。

在罚球期间,追踪裁判负责罚球线延长线后3分线外的其余的队员。

当罚球期间发生一起违例并且球在空中时,裁判员应立即鸣哨并指明违例情况(例如:罚球队员假动作)。这是为了减小违例发生后队员之间不必要的身体接触。没有必要等到球是否进入球篮。

如果球进入了球篮:

a. 罚球队员违例——中篮应不计得分。

b. 其他任意队员违例——中篮应计得分,鸣哨应被忽略,随后应如同最后一次罚球成功以掷球入界恢复比赛。

Diagram 90:
Only Centre indicates the number of free throws using the official signals.

Diagram 91: Primary responsibilities during last or only free throw.

When there is a last free-throw with opposing players in the new front court:
Trail adjusts towards the new frontcourt (position depends on the number of the players in the frontcourt and time of the game).

Diagram 92:
Trail adjusts position towards the new frontcourt during last free-throw if there is opposing players in the new front court.

图 90：
只有中央裁判做出指示罚球次数的官方手势

图 91：
在最后一次罚球或仅有一次罚球时，裁判员的责任分工

当最后一次罚球时，有双方的队员同时位于新的前场：追踪裁判应当调整他的位置移动到前场（其位置取决于前场队员的数量以及比赛的时间）。

图 92：
在最后一次罚球时，如果有双方的队员同时位于新的前场，追踪裁判应调整其位置

2.23 REBOUNDING COVERAGE

Target: To identify the correct techniques for total coverage during rebounding situations to ensure that not more than 1-2 active match-ups are covered by each referee.

For successful refereeing of rebound plays it is important to understand the principles for successful rebound techniques by the players (inside position, timing, etc.). In this section we focus on the practical implementation of these principles and how this relates to refereeing.

First of all, it is crucial to understand that when any shot is taken, this is the key moment for the players to move to the most profitable position in order to get the rebound. In many cases, referees are thinking that the key moment is when ball hits the rim, which is completely too late. Keeping in mind the key principles noted above, it is important that the referees are already in position to referee the rebound situation when the shot is taken (active mind-set, appropriate positioning for the next play). In doing so, the referee implements the basic IOT elements regarding Distance & Stationary, and active mind-set facilitating the chance to process the entire play (analytical decision) – not only to see the end and react (emotional decision).

The second successful technique is to define the principle that each referee has only 1-2 active match-ups to follow during a rebound. It is not so difficult if the referee focuses only on a few players instead of trying to cover all of the court and all the ten players. The challenge is that all referees pick-up the different match-ups. Naturally, the Pre-Game Conference plays a significant role in the correct plan, methods and execution.

Normally, each referee picks up the closest active match-up, and possibly one more. Normally, you are able to rule out one match-up that will not be active during a rebound situation that needs no active attention.

Shot from the strong side: Lead covers the match-up close to the basket (holding and clamping fouls), Trail & Centre focus on perimeter rebounds (pushing, crashing and "over-the-back") on their respective sides. Centre has primary coverage on goaltending or basket interference as Trail has shot coverage (Diagram 93).

2.23 篮板球的区域分工

目标：明确篮板球情况中整体区域分工配合的正确技巧，确保每名裁判只需负责观察 1~2 个对位。

为了成功地执裁篮板球情况，去理解成功的篮板球技术原理是很重要的（卡位和时机选择等）。在这个章节，我们将关注这些原则的实际运用以及如何能与执裁联系起来。

首先，必须明白的一点是，当投篮出手的一瞬间是队员们积极抢占有利位置拼抢篮板球的关键时刻。在众多战例中，裁判员们认为球触及篮圈的瞬间才是关键时刻，但这为时已晚。谨记上述的原则，投篮出手的时候裁判员就应该选好位置准备好对篮板球情况的监控（动态思维，为接下来的对抗选择合适的位置）。在这样做的过程中，裁判员还需执行个人执裁技术中的距离和静立原则，并通过动态思维来提供处理整个对抗全过程的机会（分析性判断），而不仅仅是看完对抗的结尾后就做出反应（情绪性判断）。

第二个成功的技巧是定义这样的原则，即每位裁判员在篮板球中只负责监控 1~2 个对位。如果裁判员只关注几名队员而不试图观察全场和场上的 10 名队员，难度就很小了。所有的裁判都分工观察不同的对位是一个挑战。当然，赛前准备对于制订合理的计划、方法和执行策略来说，扮演了十分重要的角色。

通常，每名裁判员选取最靠近他们的一对对位去观察，也有可能是两对。篮板球情况中可以不将注意力放在不存在的矛盾对位上。

强侧的投篮：前导裁判负责监控靠近球篮的对位（拉人和夹人的犯规），追踪裁判和中央裁判监控各自区域的外围篮板球（推人、撞人以及压肩背）。当追踪裁判监控投篮时，中央裁判主要负责监控干扰得分和干涉得分。（图 93）

Shot from the weak side: Lead covers the match-up close to basket (holding and clamping fouls), Trail & Centre focus on perimeter rebounds (pushing, crashing and "over-the-back") on their respective sides. Trail has primary coverage on goaltending or basket interference as Centre has shot coverage (Diagram 94).

If there are no active match-ups on your side, you need to move to the next active match-up! (not engaged with mechanics but the play & active mind-set)

Diagram 93:
Shot from the strong side, L focus on players close to basket, T & C focus on perimeter players and C has the primary for the possible goal tending and basket interference. (1) = not active match-up.

Diagram 94:
Shot from the weak side, L focus on players close to basket, T & C focus on perimeter players and T has the primary for the possible goal tending and basket interference. (1) = not active match-up.

2.24 LAST SHOT

Target: To identify which referee is on the last shot and who is responsible for controlling the game/shot clock at the end of a quarter or the game.

Normally, either the Trail or Centre decide if any shot close to the end of a quarter or game is a valid basket or if the ball was not released before the LED light/signal.

弱侧的投篮：前导裁判负责监控靠近球篮的对位（拉人或夹人的犯规），追踪裁判和中央裁判监控各自区域的外围篮板球（推人、撞人以及压肩背）。当中央裁判监控投篮时，追踪裁判主要负责监控干扰得分和干涉得分（图94）。

如果你的一侧的对位没有矛盾，你需要将视线转移到有矛盾的对位上！（不要机械式地执裁，应顺应比赛并保持动态思维）

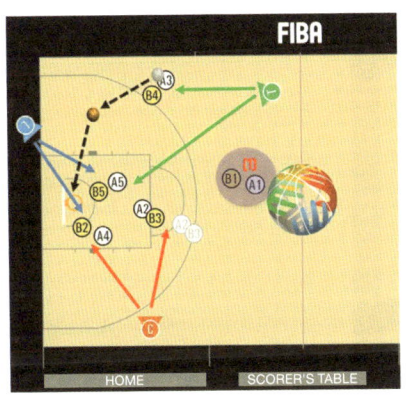

图 93：
强侧的投篮，L 监控靠近球篮的队员，T 和 C 监控外围的队员，C 主要负责监控可能出现的干扰得分和干涉得分 [1]= 没有矛盾的对位

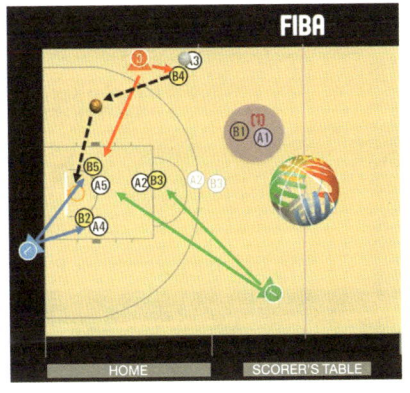

图 94：
弱侧的投篮，L 监控靠近球篮的队员，T 和 C 监控外围的队员，T 主要负责监控可能出现的干扰得分和干涉得分 [1]= 没有矛盾的对位

2.24 最后一投

目标：确认一节比赛或全场比赛的最后时刻，在最后一投中，哪名裁判员负责监控投篮，以及哪名裁判员负责控制比赛 / 进攻计时钟。

通常情况下由追踪裁判或中央裁判来决定临近一节比赛或全场比赛结束时的投篮是否有效，或者在 LED 灯亮 / 信号响之前球是否离开队员的手。

Diagram 95:
Last shot on opposite side:
- the Trail or Centre on table side (Trail or Centre) is primarily responsible for the clock (primary mode)

- the Trail or Centre (who is covering the shooting situation) on opposite side is secondarily responsible for the clock (assist mode)

Diagram 96:
Last shot on table side:
- the Trail or Centre on opposite side (Trail or Centre) is primarily responsible for the clock (primary mode)

- the Trail or Centre (who is covering the shooting situation) on table side is secondarily responsible for the clock (assist mode)

If any of the referees not covering the last shot have information regarding the last shot and the clock, they are required to go immediately to the calling referee who is responsible for the last shot and share this information with the crew (assist mode).

In the event there is disagreement amongst the crew, the Crew Chief always makes the final decision.

See also *"2.14 Control of the game and shot clock"* in FIBA Referee Manual – Individual Officiating Techniques (IOT) and "Improve your... Communication amongst the crew" publications for the correct technique and procedure.

图 95：
最后一投发生在记录台对侧：
- 记录台侧的追踪裁判或中央裁判对计时钟负主要责任（主责）

- 对侧的追踪裁判或中央裁判（正在观察投篮情况）对计时钟负次要责任（协助）

图 96：
最后一投发生在记录台侧：
- 对侧的追踪裁判或中央裁判对计时钟负主要责任（主责）

- 记录台侧的追踪裁判或中央裁判（正在观察投篮情况）对计时钟负次要责任（协助）

　　如果其他无需观察投篮情况的裁判员掌握了与最后一投以及计时钟相关的信息时，他们应立即与负责宣判最后一投的裁判员商讨，并且与整个裁判组分享相关信息（协助）。

　　当裁判员之间存在意见分歧时，主裁判负责做出最终判罚。

　　更多正确的技巧与程序参见已发布的《国际篮联裁判员手册：个人执裁技术》中"2.14 比赛和进攻计时钟的掌控"以及"提高你的……裁判员之间的沟通交流"。

第 3 章
OFFICIAL REFEREES' SIGNALS
官方裁判员手势

FIBA REFEREES MANUAL

CHAPTER 3

3. OFFICIAL REFEREES' SIGNALS

Game clock signals

STOP THE CLOCK
Open palm

STOP THE CLOCK FOR FOUL
One clenched fist

START THE CLOCK
Chop with hand

Scoring

1 POINT
1 finger, 'flag' from wrist

2 POINTS
2 fingers, 'flag' from wrist

3 POINTS
3 fingers extended
One arm: Attempt
Both arms: Successful

第3章

3. 官方裁判员手势

比赛时钟信号

停止计时钟	犯规停止计时钟	计时开始
		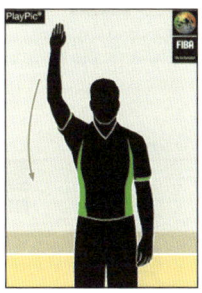
伸开手掌	一拳紧握	用手做劈砍

得分

1分	2分	3分
1指 从腕部下屈	2指 从腕部下屈	伸展3指 一只胳膊：3分试投 两只胳膊：3分投篮成功

FIBA REFEREES MANUAL

Substitution and Time-out

SUBSTITUTION	BECKONING-IN	CHARGED TIME-OUT	MEDIA TIME-OUT
Cross forearms	Open palm, wave towards the body	Form T, show index finger	Open arms with clenched fists

Informative

CANCEL SCORE, CANCEL PLAY	VISIBLE COUNT
Scissor-like action with arms, once across chest	Counting while moving the palm

COMMUNICATION	SHOT CLOCK RESET	DIRECTION OF PLAY AND/OR OUT-OF-BOUNDS	HELD BALL/JUMP BALL SITUATION
Thumb up	Rotate hand, extend index finger	Point in direction of play, arm parallel to sidelines	Thumbs up, then point in direction of play using the alternating possession arrow

替换和暂停

替换
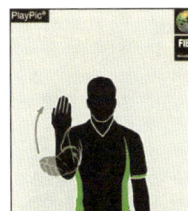
前臂交叉

招呼入场
伸出手掌
摆向身体

暂停

成"T"形
食指示之

媒体暂停
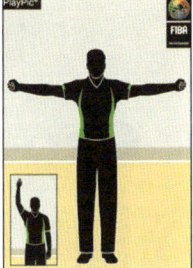
张开双臂
紧握拳头

提供信息

取消得分，中止比赛

双臂像剪的动作，胸前交叉一次

可见的计数

移动手掌计数

交流
拇指向上

进攻计时钟复位

伸出食指
并转动手

比赛方向和/或出界

指向比赛方向，
手臂与边线平行

争球/跳球情况

两拇指向上，然后
指向交替拥有箭头
所指的比赛方向

FIBA REFEREES MANUAL

Violations

TRAVELLING	ILLEGAL DRIBBLE: DOUBLE DRIBBLING	ILLEGAL DRIBBLE: CARRYING THE BALL

Rotate fists	Patting motion with palm	Half rotation with palm

3 SECONDS	5 SECONDS	8 SECONDS

  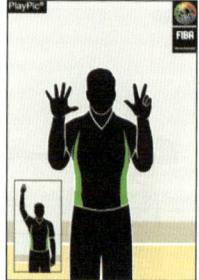

Arm extended, show 3 fingers	Show 5 fingers	Show 8 fingers

24 SECONDS	BALL RETURNED TO BACKCOURT	DELIBERATE KICK OR BLOCK OF THE BALL

  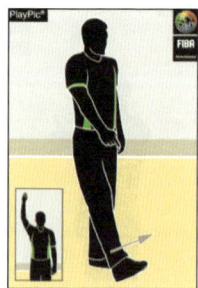

Fingers touch shoulder	Wave arm front of body	Point to the foot

违例

带球走
转动双拳

非法运球：两次运球
用手掌做轻拍动作

非法运球：携带球
半转手掌

3 秒钟
伸出手臂示 3 指

5 秒钟
示 5 指

8 秒钟
示 8 指

24 秒钟
手指触肩

球回后场
身前摆动手臂

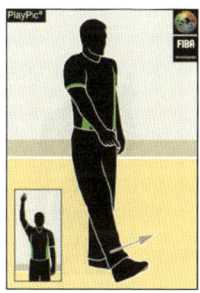
故意脚踢或拦阻球
手指指脚

101

Number of Players

No. 00 and 0

Both hands show number 0

Right hand shows number 0

No. 1 - 5

Right hand shows number 1 to 5

No. 6 - 10

Right hand shows number 5, left hand shows number 1 to 5

No. 11 - 15

Right hand shows clenched fist, left hand shows number 1 to 5

No. 16

First reverse hand shows number 1 for the decade digit - then open hands show number 6 for the units digit

No. 24

First reverse hand shows number 2 for the decade digit - then open hand shows number 4 for the units digit

队员的号码

No.00 和 No.0

双手示 0 号　　右手示 0 号

No.1-5

右手示号码 1 到 5

No.6-10

右手示 5 号，
左手示号码 1 到 5

No.11-15

右手示紧握的拳头，
左手示号码 1 到 5

No.16

首先手背朝外示 1 号代表十位数，
然后手掌朝外示 6 号代表个位数

No.24

首先手背朝外示 2 号代表十位数，
然后手掌朝外示 4 号代表个位数

FIBA REFEREES MANUAL

No. 40

First reverse hand shows number 4 for the decade digit - then open hand shows number 0 for the units digit

No. 62

First reverse hands show number 6 for the decade digit - then open hand shows number 2 for the units digit

No. 78

First reverse hands show number 7 for the decade digit - then open hands show number 8 for the units digit

No. 99

First reverse hands show number 9 for the decade digit - then open hands show number 9 for the units digit

Type of Fouls

HOLDING	BLOCKING (DEFENSE), ILLEGAL SCREEN (OFFENSE)	PUSHING OR CHARGING WITHOUT THE BALL	HANDCHECKING
Grasp wrist downward	Both hands on hips	Imitate push	Grab palm and forward motion

No.40

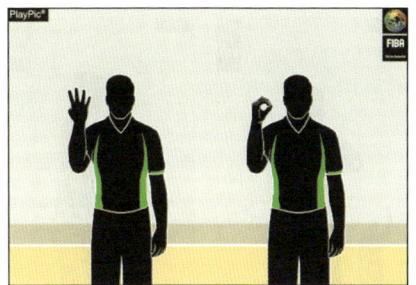

首先手背朝外示 4 号代表十位数，
然后手掌朝外示 0 号代表个位数

No.62

首先手背朝外示 6 号代表十位数，
然后手掌朝外示 2 号代表个位数

No.78

首先手背朝外示 7 号代表十位数，
然后手掌朝外示 8 号代表个位数

No.99

首先手背朝外示 9 号代表十位数，
然后手掌朝外示 9 号代表个位数

犯规的类型

拉人

向下抓住手腕

阻挡（防守）
非法掩护（进攻）

双手置髋部

推人或
不带球撞人

模仿推

用手推挡

抓住手掌向前移动

FIBA REFEREES MANUAL

ILLEGAL USE OF HANDS	CHARGING WITH THE BALL	ILLEGAL CONTACT TO THE HAND	HOOKING
Strike wrist	Clenched fist strike open palm	Strike the palm towards the other forearm	Move lower arm backwards

EXCESSIVE SWINGING OF ELBOW	HIT TO THE HEAD	FOUL BY TEAM IN CONTROL OF THE BALL
Swing elbow backwards	Imitate the contact to the head	Point clenched fist towards basket of offending team

FOUL ON THE ACT OF SHOOTING	FOUL NOT ON THE ACT OF SHOOTING
One arm with clenched fist, followed by indication of the number of free throws	One arm with clenched fist, followed by pointing to the floor

非法用手	带球撞人	对手的非法接触	勾人犯规
			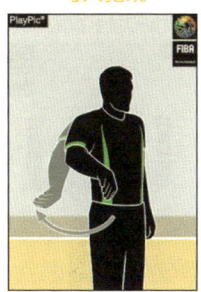
击腕	握拳击掌	掌击另一只前臂	向后移动前臂

过分挥肘	击头	控制球队的犯规
		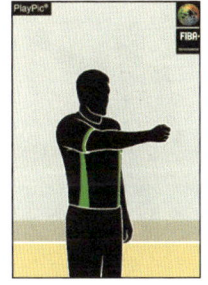
向后摆肘	模仿拍击头部	握拳指向犯规队的球篮

对投篮动作的犯规	对非投篮动作的犯规
单臂握拳举起，随后指示罚球次数	单臂握拳举起，随后指向地面

Special Fouls

DOUBLE FOUL	TECHNICAL FOUL	UNSPORTSMANLIKE FOUL	DISQUALIFYING FOUL

Wave clenched fists on both hands	Form T, showing palms	Grasp wrist upward	Clenched fists on both hands

FAKE A FOUL	ILLEGAL BOUNDARY LINE CROSSING ON A THROW-IN	IRS REVIEW

Raise the lower arm twice	Wave arm parallel to boundary line (in last 2 minutes of the fourth quarter and overtime)	Rotate hand with horizontal extended index finger

Foul Penalty Administration – Reporting to Table

AFTER FOUL WITHOUT FREE THROW(S)	AFTER FOUL BY TEAM IN CONTROL OF THE BALL

Point in direction of play, arm parallel to sidelines	Clenched fist in direction of play, arm parallel to sidelines

特殊犯规

双方犯规

挥动紧握的双拳

技术犯规

成"T"形手掌示之

违反体育运动精神的犯规

向上抓住手腕

取消比赛资格的犯规
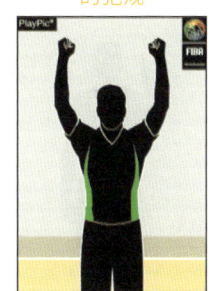
紧握双拳

骗取犯规
前臂上抬两次
（从高处做起）

掷球入界非法越线

平行于界线摆动手臂（第 4 节和决胜期最后 2:00 分钟）

调用即时回放系统

水平伸直食指转动手

向记录台报告罚则

没有罚球的犯规后

指向比赛方向，手臂与边线平行

控制球队犯规后

握拳指向比赛方向手臂与边线平行

1 FREE THROW	2 FREE THROWS	3 FREE THROWS
Hold up 1 finger	Hold up 2 fingers	Hold up 3 fingers

Administrating Free Throws – Active Referee (Lead)

1 FREE THROW	2 FREE THROWS	3 FREE THROWS
1 finger horizontal	2 fingers horizontal	3 fingers horizontal

Administrating Free Throws – Passive Referee (Trail in 2PO & Centre in 3PO)

1 FREE THROW	2 FREE THROWS	3 FREE THROWS
Index finger	Fingers together on both hands	3 fingers extended on both hands

1次罚球	2次罚球	3次罚球
举起1指	举起2指	举起3指

罚球管理—执行裁判（前导裁判）

1次罚球	2次罚球	3次罚球
水平伸1指	水平伸2指	水平伸3指

罚球管理—非执行裁判（2人执裁之追踪裁判与3人执裁之中央裁判）

1次罚球	2次罚球	3次罚球
伸食指	双手手指并拢	双手伸展3指

NOTE